Transport through the Ages

Mark Lambert

Macdonald/Silver Burdett

Editorial Manager	Chester Fisher
Senior Editor	Judith Maxwell
Editors	Bridget Daly
	Brenda Clarke
Series Designers	QED (Alaistair Campbell and Edward Kinsey)
Designers	Jim Marks and Nigel Osborne
Series Consultant	Keith Lye
Consultant	Tony Osman
Production	Penny Kitchenham
Picture Research	Leonora Elford and Janice Croot

© Macdonald Educational Ltd, 1979
First Published 1979
Macdonald Educational
Holywell House
Worship Street
London EC2A 2EN

Published in the
United States by
Silver Burdett Company
Morristown, N.J.
1980 Printing
ISBN 0-382-06410-0

World of Knowledge

This book breaks new ground in the method it uses to present information to the reader. The unique page design combines narrative with an alphabetical reference section and it uses colourful photographs, diagrams and illustrations to provide an instant and detailed understanding of the book's theme. The main body of information is presented in a series of chapters that cover, in depth, the subject of this book. At the bottom of each page is a reference section which gives, in alphabetical order, concise articles which define, or enlarge on, the topics discussed in the chapter. Throughout the book, the use of SMALL CAPITALS in the text directs the reader to further information that is printed in the reference section. The same method is used to cross-reference entries within each reference section. Finally, there is a comprehensive index at the end of the book that will help the reader find information in the text, illustrations and reference sections. The quality of the text, and the originality of its presentation, ensure that this book can be read both for enjoyment and for the most up-to-date information on the subject.

Contents

Chariots and Coaches   3
The wheel was one of man's most brilliant inventions. In the field of transport, it led to the development of war chariots, wagons for hauling supplies and, later, coaches for carrying passengers.

Across the Oceans   6
Early sailors faced great dangers when their fragile craft were swept beyond the sight of land. But, today, modern navies and shipping lines provide essential services, even in an age of fast air transport.

Travelling by Road   17
In developed countries, a car is regarded by many families not as a luxury but as a necessity. Yet the technology of mass production, which made cars cheap to buy, was introduced only in the first decade of this century.

Canals   30
Most canal construction ended when the golden age of the railways began. But some canals, such as the Panama Canal, the St Lawrence Seaway and the Suez Canal, are still vital arteries of world trade.

The Railway Revolution   33
In 1829 George Stephenson's locomotive, the *Rocket*, reached the then unheard of speed of 58 km/hour. Today Japanese 'lightning trains' reach 210 km/hour, providing the world's fastest regular service.

Travelling through Air   49
The mastery of flight, one of man's earliest dreams, is another remarkable story of technological progress. It has culminated in the supersonic airliner and rockets, which are now probing the secrets of space.

Hovercraft and Hydrofoils   62
The hovercraft is one of the most adaptable of all forms of transport, because it can travel over land and water. The air-cushion principle has many applications. It has even been used for lawn mowers.

Index   65

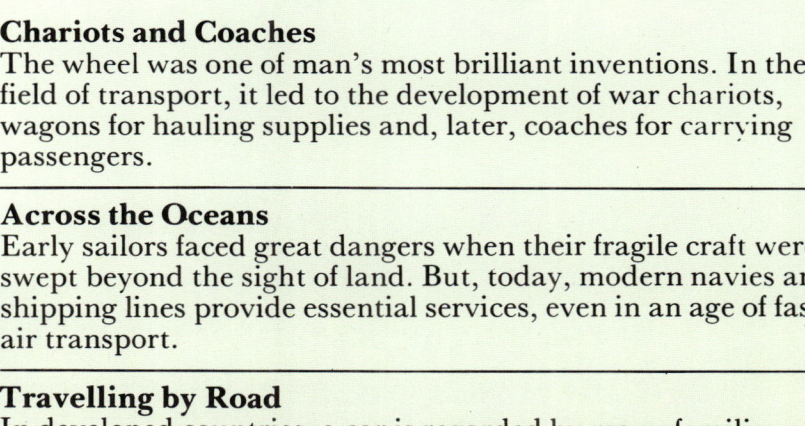

Introduction

Travel was once slow, uncomfortable and often dangerous. As a result, it was usually undertaken only when it was absolutely necessary. Transport by land and water became important as early civilizations arose. But it was the Industrial Revolution which triggered off the most rapid developments in transport, because industrialization would have been impossible without cheap and easy methods of moving bulky loads of raw materials, manufactures and foods around the world. The extent of the recent transport revolution is exemplified in the fact that, 200 years ago, it took a month or more to sail from Europe to the Americas while, in 1977, the Anglo-French supersonic airliner *Concorde* took only 3 hours and 42 minutes to fly from London to Barbados. **Transport through the Ages** tells the fascinating story of how the application of scientific principles has enabled inventors to discover ways of carrying products and people around at high speeds in comfort and safety, even beyond the Earth into space.

The wheel was one of man's most brilliant inventions. In the field of transport, it led to the development of war chariots, wagons for hauling supplies and, later, coaches for carrying passengers.

Chariots and Coaches

The early evolution of the wheel remains obscure. Possibly it developed from the use of tree trunks by Stone Age men as rollers to transport the massive stones we now find in structures such as Stonehenge and in megalithic (large stone) tombs. Gradually, men would have worked out that the central part of the roller was unnecessarily thick. From this idea it was a short step to making solid wooden wheels jammed firmly on to long axles. Such wheels could be fitted underneath a sledge with pegs to keep the axles in place. Drawings on clay tablets show that the Sumerians had these wagons in 3250 BC.

The oldest wheels that have been discovered intact come from tombs dating from 3000 to 2000 BC. They were made from three pieces of wood clamped together with cross-struts. At the same time, people learned that such light wheels could be made to turn on axles that were fixed to the wagon. The advantage of this was that the wheels on either side could turn at different speeds. Therefore, the wagon could turn corners more easily, without the outside wheels skidding and scraping along the ground. Pegs in the ends of the axles prevented the wheels from falling off. The Sumerians also found that they could prevent wooden wheels from wearing down by studding them with copper nails or by fitting bronze or leather tyres to them. When the tyre wore out, it could easily be replaced without having to make and fit new wheels.

These early wagons were simple in construction and were generally pulled by slow-moving beasts, such as oxen. However, as well as farming, the people of the early Mesopotamian civilizations were much concerned with warfare.

Below left: In the Stone Age people probably used logs as rollers to transport heavy weights.

Below: The development of the wheel. At first, solid wheels were probably cut from logs. However, such wheels break easily and stronger wheels were therefore constructed from several pieces of wood. Finally, spoked wheels combined both strength and lightness.

Reference

A **Arcera** was a Roman, 4-wheeled passenger wagon designed to be used for the sick. It was probably very uncomfortable and it was abandoned in favour of the litter — a bed carried on the shoulders of slaves.

B **Barouche** (1800s) was a 4-wheeled open carriage with a high driving seat.
Berlin coaches (1600s–1800s) were the first really successful light coaches. They had C-shaped steel springs and leather straps to help support the body. The bottom of the body was curved and bounced up and down instead of swaying from side to side. The front wheels were smaller than those at the rear, which allowed the coach to turn sharply without scraping the wheels against the body. The first Berlins only held 2 people, but later versions carried 4.
Brougham (1800s) was a popular 4-wheeled carriage drawn by 1 horse. It was designed originally by Lord Brougham for his own use.
Buggy (1800s) was a 4-wheeled vehicle used in America. It was light, easily driven and durable, and its body was supported by 2 elliptical steel springs.

C **Cabriolet** (1800s) was a 2-wheeled carriage drawn by 1 horse. It had been developed from the CHAISE and was used for hire (hence 'cab').
Chaise (1700s) was an open 2-wheeled carriage drawn by 1 horse. It had wooden springs and a folding roof. In America it was known as the Shay.
Char, or Curré (1300s), was a 4-wheeled wagon used by queens and duchesses in France. It had been very popular during the 1200s, but in 1294 Philip II forbade its use by the wives of the bourgeoisie. Its body rested directly on the axles. Fixed

Undersprung step-piece barouche, 1851

Above: Solid wheels are still used in some countries. The wheels of these Vietnamese carts have been constructed in much the same way for thousands of years.

The Sumerians had learned to control wild asses (onagers) and used them to pull their war chariots. Then it was discovered that horses could pull chariots even faster. This encouraged people to try to make their wagons lighter and, in about 2000 BC, the spoked wheel was invented somewhere in eastern Iran. At first, such wheels had only four SPOKES surrounded by a thick rim. However, the number of spokes was soon increased, therefore allowing the rim to be made thinner and lighter, without reducing the strength of the wheel. The use of spoked wheels spread rapidly into Mesopotamia. The warlike Assyrians used them not only for their chariots, but also for gigantic, turreted battering rams.

The early Sumerian chariots were four-wheelers and, although the wheels ran independently, they were difficult to steer round corners. Two-wheeled chariots did not have this problem and were lighter and faster. The Egyptians, who received the spoked wheel and the horse from Mesopotamia in about 1600 BC, used two-wheelers to great advantage in battle.

By this time the RIMS of wheels were being covered in copper. This is a fairly soft metal and, like the leather rims used by the Sumerians, quickly wore away. However, in northern Europe in 700 BC, the Celts were using iron rims for their wheels. They made an iron hoop, slightly smaller than the wheel. When this was heated, it expanded until it could be slipped over the wheel. Cooling the iron 'tyre' caused it to contract and grip the wheel tightly. So the tread of the wheel was made tougher, and the whole wheel became stronger.

The Romans, with their vast empire, needed fast communications and this encouraged them to build good roads and to improve the available means of transport. They copied many of the Celtic ideas and the best Roman wagons had iron-tyred wheels with metal-lined hubs. The cornering ability of a four-wheeled wagon was also improved by placing the front axle on a pivot so that it could be steered. In addition, the Romans also used a double shaft instead of a single pole. This meant that light carts could be pulled by one horse rather than two.

After the decline of the Roman Empire, European roads were neglected, but travel continued to increase. Horses were fitted with iron shoes and harnesses that did not strangle them. Wagons with a form of suspension appeared. The body of the wagon was built as a separate box and hung on chains or leather straps from four posts attached to the chassis. This reduced the jolting, but unfortunately some

to the front axle there was either a pole (if the horses were to be attached in pairs) or two shafts (if the horses were to be in tandem). It was mainly built of wood, but many of the fittings were of iron and the whole thing could weigh nearly 1,000 kg. As a result, the char needed 4 or 6 horses to pull it.
Concord coaches (1800s) were the famous stage-coaches of the American West. They were fast and very durable.
Conestoga wagons (1700s), also known as prairie schooners, were used in America to transport freight along the Santa Fé trail and settlers to Oregon and California. The bed of the Conestoga was about 5 metres long and the rear wheels were nearly 2 metres high. The hoops, which were covered in white canvas, stood over 3 metres from the ground. Up to 6 horses, mules or oxen were needed to pull it.
Curricle (1800s) was a 2-wheeled carriage drawn by 2 horses.

D **Diligence** was the name given in England in 1783 to mail coaches. These were BERLIN COACHES and they could travel at a speed of 11 km/hour while carrying mail and 4 passengers, but no luggage. In France the name Diligence was given to a POST-CHAISE drawn by 3 horses abreast and driven by a postillion.
Dished wheels appeared during the Middle Ages. The top of a dished wheel could be angled outwards, while the hub remained vertically above the point where the rim touched the ground. Thus the body of the wagon could be built wider, while the axle remained short enough to bear the weight.

G **Gig** (1670) was a light, 2-wheeled cart with a high chair in which the driver used to sit.

H **Hackney coaches** (1600s) were 4-wheeled vehicles used for hire.
Hansom cabs were 2-wheeled carriages used for hire. Designed by J. A. Hansom in 1834, they superseded the CABRIOLET. A hansom cab had a square, enclosed body with a seat for the driver on the roof.

L **Landau** (1700s) was a 4-wheeled carriage with a folding hood. The name Landaulet was given to smaller versions of this vehicle.

Hansom cab, 1887

passengers were made 'wagon-sick' by the swaying motion. Despite these few improvements travelling by wagon remained slow and uncomfortable for several centuries. Most people preferred the faster, pleasanter method of travelling on horseback, particularly when swift communications were needed.

In the 1500s the first coaches were built in Hungary. These resembled large bath tubs on wheels, but by the early 1600s coaches more familiar to us were being built in Germany. Some of these had glass windows and steel springs. Coaches could now go faster, but poor roads often prevented them from travelling quickly. Eventually, the invention of macadamized roads (*see page 29*) in 1810 led to the development of STAGECOACHES, the fastest of which were the mail coaches. Passengers found these much more comfortable because they had laminated spring suspension — the kind still used in some cars today. Their wheels had bolt-on hubs so that faulty or broken wheels could be replaced swiftly.

Below: A reconstruction of a Celtic chariot. In about AD 500 the Celts used to bury chariots with their owners and many metal parts have been excavated from such graves. Pictures on coins provide an idea of what such chariots looked like. A grave stone in northern Italy shows a long chariot with 2 semi-circular pieces on one side – as shown here. These were probably used as handholds by the warrior and his driver. The chariot had spoked wheels held on to the axles by linchpins. The trace reins were attached to the axle.

Left: An English stagecoach of the 1800s. First-class passengers rode inside, and second-class passengers rode on top with the coachman. The bolt-on wheels had iron rims and carved oak spokes.

P **Phaeton** (1800s) was a high, 4-wheeled carriage drawn by 1 or 2 horses. It was noted for its ability to turn corners sharply and its drivers earned the reputation of being reckless.
Post-chaise (1743) was a 2-wheeled carriage suspended on leather braces and drawn by 1 horse. Travelling post meant that the driver and horse could be changed at stations every few kilometres. Later post-chaises had 4 wheels.
R **Raeda** (reda) was a 4-wheeled Roman cart taken from the Celts, used for long-distance travel.
Rim of a spoked wheel is the outer part that makes contact with the ground. When spoked wheels were first invented the rim was made of a single piece of wood bent into shape using steam. Later rims had several pieces of wood (felloes) slotted into each other, bound with a metal tyre.
S **Sedan chairs** (1600s and 1700s) were enclosed chairs for 1 passenger only, carried by 2 men. Although they received much competition from the increasing number of coaches, they were more comfortable and so were used until the early 1800s.
Spokes are thin pieces of wood or metal that join the RIM of a wheel to the hub. The first wooden spokes were invented about 2000 BC when someone realized that an apparently thin stick will not break if a weight is applied along its length. This allowed a wheel to be both strong and light.
Stagecoaches (1800s) received their name from the fact that long journeys were broken at staging posts, usually inns, along the route. The coachmen, horses and passengers could get rest and food before continuing their journey.
W **Whirlicote** was the English name for the CHAR.

Phaeton, c.1857

Early sailors faced great dangers when their fragile craft were swept beyond the sight of land. But, today, modern navies and shipping lines provide essential services, even in an age of fast air transport.

Across the Oceans

Below: The earliest Egyptian boats were constructed from reeds of which there was a plentiful supply. The bow and stern were joined by a rope that could be tightened. By 3000 BC reed boats were journeying to Crete and Lebanon to bring back materials such as timber.

Man's natural element is the land. But even in the earliest days of civilization, curiosity probably led him to construct boats, and venture on to the water. The first boats were very simple. DUG-OUT CANOES of the type still used in some Pacific Islands were probably the earliest boats to appear. However, in order to travel long distances, more elaborate boats were needed. By

Reference

Aft is a nautical term that means near or towards the rear of a ship.
Asdic is a form of SONAR in which pulses of ultrasound are beamed out horizontally beneath the ship and the reflected echoes are converted electronically into audible sound in the form of 'pings'. By aiming the sound beam the operator can find the range and bearing of a submarine from the echoes returned by its hull. The direction and speed of the submarine's movement are detected by the pitch, or note, of the returning echoes, using the DOPPLER EFFECT.
Astrolabe was an instrument used to measure the angle between a star and the horizontal. It was suspended by a ring from one hand and the star was viewed through two small holes at each end of a movable pointer. The angle could then be read off the circular scale.

Backstaff was an instrument used to measure the angle between the Sun and the horizon at noon. A long stick, or staff, was aligned with the horizon using a slit at the end. A curved vane was then moved so that the top of its shadow aligned with the slit. The angle could then be read from the vane. By consulting his DECLINATION tables the navigator could quickly work out his latitude.
Battleship is the most heavily armed type of ship used in war and is designed to attack and defeat any other type of ship. In the 1600s to 1800s a battleship was called a SHIP-OF-THE-LINE. During World War I massive, heavily-armed and armoured ships were built, such as HMS *Dreadnought*, which carried 10 300-mm guns and had 275-mm thick armour.

Battleship HMS Dreadnought

2700 BC the Egyptians were building rafts of papyrus reeds, and their high-prowed wooden boats had begun sailing the waters of the River Nile and the Red Sea.

The early sailors did not venture far from land and so could easily find their position from landmarks along the coast. The only hazards to avoid were running aground or on to rocks. The Egyptian river boats had two men in the bows — one to test the depth of water with a long pole, the other to signal instructions to the helmsman.

Once out of sight of land, however, finding the boat's position was more difficult. With no landmarks to guide them the early seafarers had to discover new ways of finding out where they were. The Mediterranean Sea has been called 'the cradle of navigation', because it was there that sailors first ventured on to the open sea.

Below: The reed boat was basically just a raft, the natural buoyancy of the reeds keeping it afloat. To prevent the reeds from becoming waterlogged they were bound together in 2 bundles. Some drawings show reed boats with sails, which were probably made from rush matting.

The Mediterranean sailors

The Egyptians, Greeks and Phoenicians were the first to sail the Mediterranean and the earliest written record of navigation is provided by the Greek historian Herodotus. He tells us that when approaching land, sailors let down a weighted line with a lump of tallow on the end. The length of line gave the depth of water, and the gravel, sand or mud that stuck to the tallow told the experienced captain where he was. For example, yellow mud indicated that the ship was approaching the mouth of the River Nile.

Of all the Mediterranean sailors the Phoenicians were the most proficient. By about 1200 BC they had established trading posts all round the Mediterranean and had sailed into the Atlantic Ocean. They even reached the coast of Cornwall in England, where they traded with the tin

Biremes, triremes and quinqueremes were types of Greek and Roman galley. It is disputed whether these names meant that the vessels had 2, 3 or 5 banks of oars on each side or 2, 3 or 5 oarsmen to each oar. However, the latter seems likely, as in vessels with 3 or 5 banks of oars, the oarsmen on the higher levels would have had to pull impossibly long and heavy oars.

Caravel was a small, fast sailing ship, LATEEN-RIGGED except for the foremast, used mainly in the Mediterranean during the 1400s to 1600s. The *Niña* and *Pinta,* 2 of Columbus's ships, were caravels.

Carrack, or nao, was a small, broad, square-rigged merchant ship common in the 1500s. Columbus's ship *Santa Maria* was a carrack.

Carvel-built ships are made from long wooden planks with the edges of the planks butted against each other. The joints are sealed with pitch. Greek, Phoenician and Roman ships were carvel-built.

Clinker-built boats are made from long wooden planks and each plank overlaps the one below it. The Viking ships were built by this method. The technique persisted into the Middle Ages.

Cog boat, which appeared in Europe in about 1200, was the forerunner of the CARRACK and the GALLEON. It had a single square sail and a turret at each end.

Corvette is a small warship. In the 1700s a corvette was a sailing ship with a single, level deck and only 1 tier of guns. The modern corvette is an escort vessel. Corvettes used in World War II carried 2 100-mm guns, several anti-aircraft guns and anti-submarine armament.

Cross-staff was an instrument used to measure the angle between the Sun or a

French corvette, 1800s

Across the Oceans

miners. Their greatest achievement was to make the first known voyage round Africa. In about 600 BC, sailors set out from the Red Sea and worked their way round the coast. Each year they stopped, planted seed and then waited for the harvest before continuing their journey. Three years after starting out they had reached the Straits of Gibraltar.

The Phoenicians were superb navigators. They learned the importance of the stars, and Greek sailors still call the Pole Star the 'Phoenician Star'. The Greeks also learned to use the stars. In Homer's epic poem the *Odyssey*, written in about 850 BC, the hero Odysseus is described as having steered his boat by the Pleiades, Arcturus and the Great Bear.

The Greeks and Phoenicians also had formidable fighting ships. Each one was rowed by hundreds of slaves and manned with soldiers. At the bow was an underwater pointed ram for sinking enemy vessels. The Phoenicians pioneered this design of ship and the Greeks copied it, with success. At the battle of Salamis in 480 BC a mere 300 Greek galleys defeated about 1,000 Persian ships. Some 500 years later the Romans were still using a similar design of warship.

The northern sailors

When the Phoenicians visited Cornwall, they saw men who sailed to Ireland in boats made of skin. These were the Irish curraghs and Welsh coracles, which can still be seen today. But it was many centuries before the northern Europeans began to build boats to match those of the Phoenicians and Romans. When they did, some time between AD 500 and 700, they built long wooden boats, generally for warlike purposes. The European long boats eventually evolved into the Viking longships, which the fierce Viking warriors used for raiding and conquering large areas of Europe.

The navigators of the northern seas were faced with several problems not found in the Mediterranean. The weather could not be relied on to remain calm, and storms could cause waves up to about 9 metres high. The Sun and stars could not be used with such accuracy for navigation as the difference between the summer and winter risings and settings is much greater than in the Mediterranean. The greatest problem was the tide, particularly for sailors from the almost tideless Mediterranean.

The Vikings, however, overcame these problems and made long voyages across the Atlantic

Above: A Roman galley of about AD 50. In battle the main form of propulsion was by oars, but if there was a favourable wind the sails could be used on long trips. The wooden ram was bound with iron or bronze and used for sinking enemy ships.

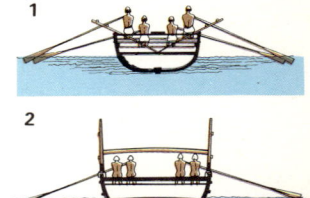

Above: It is disputed whether the term bireme meant two banks of oars (**1**) or two men to each oar (**2**). The latter would seem to be more likely. In a trireme or quinqireme, if there had been three or five banks of oars, the top bank would have had oars that were too long and heavy for the oarsmen to manage.

---

star and the horizon. It consisted of a long stick, or staff, which was aligned with the horizon, and a small crosspiece which could be lined up with the Sun or star by sliding it along the staff. The required angle could be read from a scale along the staff.
Cruiser is a warship designed for speed. During World War I there were several classes of cruiser, which varied in displacement and armament according to the work they were required for.

D Decca is a navigation system that uses radio signals transmitted by a master station and 3 slave stations. The navigator chooses the 2 most convenient slaves and the Decca receiver indicates the 2 time differences between the arrival of the master signal and the arrival of the 2 slave signals. These time differences can be plotted along curved position lines on a chart. In practice the lines are already plotted and where the 2 position lines cross is the ship's position. Decca only works within 160 km of the transmitting stations. *See also* DECTRA, LORAN.

Declination of the Sun or a star is its angular distance north or south of the equator. At the equinoxes (21 March and 21 September) the Sun is immediately above the equator and its declination is therefore zero. On any other day the Sun's declination can be found from the *Nautical Almanack*. To find the ship's latitude when it is on the opposite side of the equator to the Sun the declination has to be subtracted from the ZENITH distance (90° less the instrument-measured angular altitude of the Sun). When the ship and Sun are on the same side of the equator the declination is added to the zenith distance.
Dectra is a navigation system that uses radio sig-

Destroyer HMS Glasgow

Across the Oceans

Above: A portion of the Bayeux Tapestry, which tells the story of the Norman invasion of Britain in 1066. Here, the Norman fleet is setting sail from the French coast. They had square-rigged ships, each with a single sail. The steering oar on the starboard side of the ship is clearly shown.

Ocean. They used 'homing' winds to carry them where they wanted to go; in summer easterly winds carried them across to Iceland and Greenland; and by sailing south they could pick up prevailing westerly winds to carry them home. It is also generally believed that the Vikings reached America. Leif Eriksson, a Norwegian explorer, set out to find a land previously sighted by accident. He found it and after spending the winter there, returned home loaded with grapes. He therefore named the land Vinland, which is generally thought to have been what is now known as Newfoundland.

Sailors of the Pacific Ocean

As the Polynesians spread into the Pacific islands from Asia they were faced with the problem of sailing vast distances in their frail canoes. Even the larger double canoes, called *tonkiaka* or *kalia*, were vulnerable in really bad weather. As a result the Polynesians became sensitive to the weather and could forecast fairly accurately up to three days ahead.

They also developed navigation into a sophisticated art. In many of the islands, navigation schools were set up. There, young men were taught how to steer by the stars and how to recognize indicators of land, such as wave motions, cloud colours and birds. On the Isle of Arorae they were shown how to use DIRECTION STONES to determine the directions of nearby islands.

There were also a few navigational aids. In the Marshall Islands the natives had elaborate TWIG CHARTS to show the distance and bearings of other islands. In Hawaii there was an instrument called a SACRED CALABASH, which enabled the navigator to find out when his boat reached the same LATITUDE as the island.

Compasses and charts

Until AD 1000 navigation was mostly a matter of observation, memory, guesswork and luck. The scientific and mathematical skills of the Greeks had been denied to western Europe by the Church, which regarded them as black magic. However, they had been handed down to the Syrians and from them to the Arabs and by now were beginning to have more influence in Europe.

The compass, originally invented by the Chinese 1,000 years before, now reappeared in Europe. To begin with it took the form of a magnetic needle inside a straw, which was floated in a bowl of water. By 1180 sailors were using a needle on a pivot. This arrangement was later improved by mounting the needle on a card and pivoting them both together. Therefore, although it seemed like magic at the time, sailors could determine the approximate direction of the North Pole under any conditions.

The charts of the 1400s were far from accurate. Distance was very difficult to measure. Little was known of magnetic VARIATION or DEVIATION and

Right: A lateen-rigged Arab dhow. Such boats have been in use for over 1,500 years. In about AD 500 the Arabs were using seasonal monsoon winds to sail to India and back.

---

nals. It works in a similar way to DECCA, but is used for transatlantic crossings. There is a master and slave pair of transmitters in England and another pair in Newfoundland. The 2 pairs transmit signals alternately and by comparing their times of arrival and the time difference between the master and slave signals, the receiver indicates the ship's position. The Dectra system uses longer wavelengths (up to 1 km) than the Decca system and works over distances of up to 1,600 km.

Destroyer is an abbreviation for torpedo-boat destroyer. In World War I they were especially useful in combating U-boats (German submarines) after the development of the depth charge. Modern destroyers carry guided missiles.

Deviation is the amount by which a compass needle is deflected by the magnetic field caused by the metal and electrical parts of a ship.

Direction stones on the Isle of Arorae were used by the Polynesians to indicate the direction of nearby islands. Each stone had 2 poles set into it and a navigator setting off in the evening could take his course by aligning the poles. By the time they were out of sight it was dark and he could steer by the stars.

Doppler effect is used in ASDIC and in RADAR and satellite navigation. Sound or radio waves emitted by or reflected from a moving object change in frequency. If the source and receiver are moving towards each other, the frequency increases, and, in the case of asdic, a higher note is heard. If the source and receiver are moving away from each other the frequency decreases.

Dug-out canoes were the first form of boat. They were made from solid logs hollowed out with either tools or fire. Such boats appeared in many parts of the world and are still used in some places. Stability was achieved by placing stones

Peruvian Indians making dug-out canoe

Below: Ship development from the 1400s to 1600s.
1. Columbus's ship *Niña* was a caravel. When he sailed from Palos the *Niña* was lateen rigged, as shown here. However, she was rerigged with square sails in the Canary Islands.
2. A two-masted carrack of the mid-1400s. Columbus's ship *Santa Maria* was a similar vessel except that she had three masts.
3. A Spanish galeass of the mid-1500s, a type of ship obviously derived from the Roman galley.
4. *Ark Royal* was one of the English galleons that fought the Spanish Armada in 1588.
5. *Henry Grâce à Dieu*, a French galleon built in the 1540s.

taking correct bearings was therefore almost impossible. Charts were also very difficult to use because converting the sphere of the world on to a flat chart led to several distortions.

The problems were, to some extent, solved by Gerardus MERCATOR. He devised a new, flat projection of the world on which a straight line represented the true course between two points. Although the sizes of Greenland and Antarctica were greatly exaggerated on such MERCATOR PROJECTIONS, this did not concern the early navigators as they avoided these regions anyway. Unfortunately, Mercator's maps were not published until 1585, so they were not available to the great explorers.

The great age of exploration

In the early 1400s, the prospect of finding gold, spices, silks and new trade routes was a great incentive to the first explorers and the merchants who financed them. Spices were to be found in India, but the land routes had been closed by the expansion of the Ottoman Turk empire. Therefore men began to look for a sea route to India. Prince Henry of Portugal, also known as Henry the Navigator (1394–1460), set up a school at Sagres, and gathered together astronomers, mathematicians, navigators, masters, shipbuilders and instrument makers. By 1446 the Portuguese had reached the Azores and Madeira, and in 1461 they landed in Sierra Leone on the West African coast. In 1487, Bartholomew Diaz sailed round the southern tip of Africa, rediscovering the route sailed by the Phoenicians 2,000 years earlier. His crew forced him to turn back, but in 1498 Vasco da Gama reached India by this route.

By this time most European scholars believed that the Earth was round. However, 1° on the equator was thought to equal 90 kilometres. From this Christopher Columbus (1451–1506), an Italian explorer, estimated that the Earth's circumference was 32,830 kilometres and that Asia lay 4,800 kilometres away across the Atlantic Ocean. His plans for making the voyage were rejected by the Portuguese and English, but on 3 August 1492 he set sail with the *Santa Maria*, *Niña* and *Pinta*, with the blessing of the King and Queen of Spain. On 12 October, Columbus landed at San Salvador in the Bahamas, believing that he had reached Asia. From there he sailed on to Cuba, which he mistook for Japan. Columbus made three more voyages to the West Indies and was for a time Governor of Hispaniola, but when he died he was still unaware that he had reached America and not Asia.

The land that lay beyond the West Indies was

in the bottom or by lashing 2 canoes together.

Fore-and-aft rigged ships are those with sails, usually triangular, set lengthwise to the ship. *See also* SQUARE-RIGGED.

Frigate is a medium-sized warship. In the 1700s it was a sailing ship that carried between 28 and 60 guns, but was not a SHIP-OF-THE-LINE. Today the term is loosely used to mean a CRUISER or large CORVETTE.

Galleon was the large type of sailing ship that developed from the CARRACK towards the end of the

French frigate Hercule, *1700s*

1500s. It was slimmer, lower and faster than the carrack and had 3 to 4 masts and several levels of upper deck. The galleon design was used for both merchant ships and warships for 250 years.

Gyrocompass always points towards True North. This is because once the spinning gyroscope in its specially weighted frame has been aligned with the Earth's axis, it maintains this orientation despite changes in direction of the ship.

Inertial guidance system uses gyroscopes to detect all the movements of a ship, i.e. speeding up, slowing down, starting, stopping and changing direction. The gyroscopes feed the information into a computer and, if the starting position of the ship is known, the computer can work out the ship's position at any time.

Kamal was a simple Arab instrument for estimating LATITUDE. It consisted of a piece of card with a hole in the centre and a notch at the top. Attached to the middle of the card was a piece of string along which knots were tied at regular intervals. The navigator held the string in his mouth and sighted a known star through the notch. He then allowed the string to slip through his teeth until the hole in the centre of the card was aligned with the horizon. From the number of knots between his mouth and the card he could then work out his latitude.

Lateen-rigged ships had one or more triangular sails, each of which was suspended from a long yard

first recognized as a new continent by the Italian Amerigo Vespucci (1451–1512), and eventually it was named after him rather than Columbus. Vespucci claimed to have made four voyages to the Americas, and in 1497 John Cabot, a Venetian, rediscovered Newfoundland. But it was left to Ferdinand Magellan, a Portuguese explorer, to find the sea route to Asia. In 1519 he sailed from Cadiz with five ships and eventually found his way through the narrow straits at the southern end of South America, now known as the Straits of Magellan. He was therefore the first to sail westwards into the Pacific Ocean. However, he never returned to Spain as he was killed by natives on the island of Mactan in the Philippines. In 1522 only one of Magellan's ships, the *Victoria*, returned to Spain, via the Moluccas and the Cape of Good Hope. This journey was not repeated for 50 years. In 1577 the English adventurer Sir Francis Drake in the *Golden Hind* set out on a voyage, the stated purpose of which was to open up the spice trade. His secret mission was to discover *Terra Australis Incognita* (now Australia) and to raid Spanish settlements and ships. He failed to find the southern continent, but in 1580 he returned to England laden with £10 million worth of plunder, having also completed the second voyage round the world.

Above: A map of Europe and the Atlantic Ocean drawn by Bartolomeo Pareto in 1455. Europe and North Africa are shown relatively accurately, and cold, white lands are described in the north. But the land to the west, named 'Antillia', is pure imagination.

(wooden pole) attached to the mast at an angle of 45°. Lateen-rigged ships are still used, for example in Arab dhows, but in Europe they were replaced by SQUARE-RIGGED ships. However, lateen sails were the forerunner of the modern FORE-AND-AFT sails used in yachts.

Latitude of a point on the Earth's surface is its angular distance, north or south of the equator, measured from the centre of the Earth. Thus the equator is 0° latitude, the North Pole is 90°N, and the South Pole is 90°S. Any line on the Earth's surface parallel to the equator is a line of latitude and the circular lines of latitude decrease in circumference from the equator to the poles.

Log and line was an instrument used from the 1400s to measure the speed of a ship. It consisted of a weighted, triangular piece of wood, or log chip, on the end of a line. Along the line there were knots every 13 metres. The log chip was thrown over the stern of the ship and the line paid out freely for 30 seconds. Then it was hauled in and the number of knots that had passed over the ship's stern was the speed in NAUTICAL MILES per hour, or knots. The log and line was replaced by the PATENT LOG in the 1700s.

Longitude of a point on the Earth's surface is the angular distance east or west of the PRIME MERIDIAN measured from the centre of the Earth. The easiest way to measure longitude is by time; 1 hour of time equals 15° of longitude. Therefore if the time in London at 0° longitude is 12.00 noon and the time in New Orleans is 6.00 a.m. the difference is 6 hours and New Orleans is at 90°W.

Loran (*L*ong *ra*nge *n*avigation) is a navigation system that works on the same principle as DECCA and DECTRA. All three systems work by comparing the times of arrival of radio waves at a receiver. In the Loran system the waves are viewed on a screen, like that of a television. A dial is turned so that the waves coincide on the screen and the time difference is read from the dial. Like the Decca system, Loran uses long wavelengths and has a range of up to 1,280 km.

0° meridian marker

M Mercator, Gerardus (1512–94) was a Flemish geographer, born Gerhard Kremer. His first

Across the Oceans

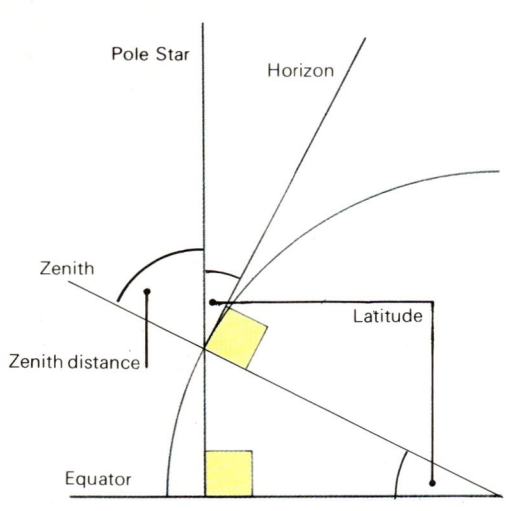

Far left: The latitude of any point on the Earth's surface is the angle at the centre of the Earth between a line drawn from that point and a line drawn from the equator.

Left: The same angle of latitude can be found by measuring the angle between the Pole Star and the horizon. During the day the angle between the Sun and the horizon can be measured. Latitude is found by adding or subtracting the declination of the Sun from the zenith distance (*see* DECLINATION).

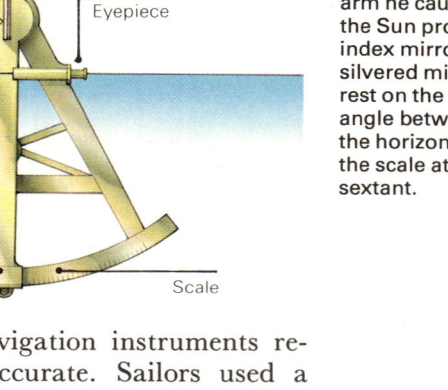

Left: Using a cross-staff to measure the angle between the Sun and the horizon.

Left: A sextant. The navigator lines up the eyepiece and the half-silvered mirror with the horizon. Then by moving the arm he causes the image of the Sun produced by the index mirror and the half-silvered mirror to appear to rest on the horizon. The angle between the Sun and the horizon can be read from the scale at the bottom of the sextant.

During this time navigation instruments remained somewhat inaccurate. Sailors used a system known as dead reckoning to work out their position by estimating the direction and distance they had sailed since the last known position. They used a TRAVERSE BOARD to tell the pilot in what direction and for how long they had sailed and judged the speed of their ship by using a LOG AND LINE. Finding the ship's position was difficult. LATITUDE, or the ship's distance from the equator, was found by measuring the angle between the Sun or Pole Star and the horizon. For this there was the Arab KAMAL or the European CROSS-STAFF, BACKSTAFF, ASTROLABE and QUADRANT. If conditions were right for using such instruments, the navigator could estimate his latitude to within 32 kilometres.

Finding the ship's LONGITUDE was even more difficult. From the late 1400s it had been realized that knowing the correct time was important. Navigators compared the observed (ship's) time of certain astronomical events, such as eclipses of planets by the Moon or the position of the Sun at noon, with the times for such events recorded on land. However, the ship's clocks and hour-glasses of the time were far too inaccurate. In 1714 the Board of Longitude was set up and a prize of £20,000 was offered to anyone who could devise an accurate method of finding longitude at sea. In 1729 John Harrison, a surveyor, set to work to produce a marine clock. Over the next 31 years he built three clocks, none of which completely satisfied the Board. But in 1761 he produced a watch-style chronometer that was taken on a trip to the West Indies and back. After the 147-day voyage the watch was only 1 minute 54 seconds in error. On a later trip it only lost 15 seconds.

Replicas of Harrison's chronometer were taken by Captain Cook on his voyages of exploration in *Resolution*. He could determine his position so

contribution to navigation was to make accurate globes with lines of latitude and MERIDIANS of longitude marked on them. These became available to navigators in 1541. Until this time men had been influenced by Greek geography, particularly Ptolemy's map of the world, which was somewhat inaccurate and included only Europe and Asia. With the discovery of new lands it became less easy to depict the world on a flat map until Mercator solved the problem with his MERCATOR PROJECTION.

Mercator projection is also known as a cylindrical projection. Imagine a cylinder of paper placed round a globe at the centre of which there is a light. The light casts a shadow of the Earth's surface on to the cylinder. When this is unwrapped it carries a map of the world on which the MERIDIANS of LONGITUDE are vertical and parallel and the lines of LATITUDE are horizontal and parallel. As one moves north or south away from the equator the lines of latitude spread out and Greenland and Antarctica are enlarged. A straight line on such a map does not necessarily represent the true distance between two points, but it does represent the true course – a much more important factor in navigation. On other projections the true course is represented by a curved line.

Meridian is a line of LONGITUDE that runs from the North to the South Pole.

Nautical mile is equal to 1.151 statute miles (6,076 ft or 1,852 metres). It is different from a statute mile because navigators have always calculated their position on the Earth's surface in degrees and it is therefore easier to measure the distance between two points in round numbers of degrees; 60 nautical miles equal 1°. However, until the 1600s, due to miscalculation of the Earth's circumference, the nautical mile was reckoned as 1,524 metres and the LOG AND LINE used the short knot of 13 metres. In 1635 the nautical mile was more accurately estimated as 1,853 metres and the knot as 15.5 metres. Even so the short knot was still being used in the 1800s. Modern instruments have allowed the nautical mile to be calculated to its present very high

Gerardus Mercator

Right: Brunel's steamship, the *Great Eastern,* which was completed in 1858. It was the largest steamship of its time and could carry 4,000 passengers or 10,000 troops. Altogether, 10,200 tonnes of iron and 5,430 square metres of canvas were used in its construction.

precisely that he was able to produce extremely accurate charts, some of which are still used today. The accuracy of Cook's navigation was further assisted by the work of Edmund Halley, generally better known for his discovery of Halley's Comet. He observed how his compass varied by different amounts from True North in different parts of the world. From this work came the first isogonic charts, which gave sailors the magnetic VARIATION in any part of the world. With such information they were then able to take accurate bearings.

The invention of two more instruments helped to improve navigation. One of these, the PATENT LOG, was a small brass cylinder used to record the distance sailed. It is still used on ocean voyages. But the instrument that was most important in making navigation easier was the SEXTANT. This instrument is still used to determine accurately a ship's latitude by finding the angle between the horizon and the Sun or, at night, a star. By using a sextant and a chronometer a navigator can pinpoint his position on the Earth's surface.

Left: The *Charlotte Dundas* is known as the first successful steamboat. She was built in 1801 for Lord Dundas and named after his wife. In March 1803 she towed 2 loaded vessels along the Forth and Clyde Canal. However, further trips were prevented by the owners of the canal. They were afraid that the wash from the paddle wheel would damage the canal banks.

degree of accuracy.

Nocturnal was an instrument used in the 1500s and 1600s for finding local time at sea. It was a form of circular slide rule and had a fixed outer scale marked with dates and a movable inner scale marked with times and with two 'ears'. One ear was for use with the Great Bear (Plough) constellation, the other with the Little Bear. Pivoted in the middle was a long arm. The navigator set the Great Bear 'ear' to the correct date on the outer scale and sighted the Pole Star through the hole in the middle of the instrument. Then he moved the arm so that it lined up with the pointers of the Great Bear. The time was shown where the arm crossed the inner scale.

O Octant was invented in 1731 by John Hadley. It was the forerunner of the SEXTANT, but the arm could move through an arc of only 45° and therefore the maximum angle that could be measured was 90°.

P Patent log was a small brass cylinder with fins to make it rotate when towed in the water behind a ship. Each rotation caused dials on the side of the cylinder to record the distance the ship had travelled. Early patent logs were not very accurate and contrary currents and surging movements of the ship caused them to record greater distances than had actually been travelled. Later patent logs had a recording clock on board ship and a brass flywheel that evened out the surges of speed. Patent logs are still used on ocean voyages and the distance is recorded electronically.

Port is the left-hand side of a ship when looking towards the bow. The origin of the

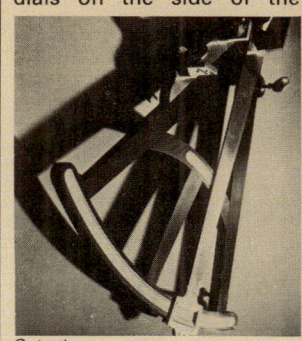

Octant

term is uncertain. Formerly it was known as larboard, which may have been due to the fact that the ship was loaded, or laden, with cargo from the side nearest the port dock. *See also* STARBOARD.

Prime meridian, 0° LONGITUDE, is the MERIDIAN that passes through a point at the ROYAL OBSERVATORY, Greenwich, London. During the late 1700s and early 1800s each country recognized a different position for 0° longitude: the French, Paris; the Italians, Rome; and so on. But in 1844 a congress met

From sail to modern ships

The sailing ships used by the great explorers were developed from the European long boats. But for about 500 years the design of sailing ships changed very little. Wide, three- or four-masted ships with large, square sails were a familiar sight on the oceans of the world. The Spanish Armada (1588) and the fleets that fought in the battle of Trafalgar (1805) were composed of ships similar to those of Columbus. In the early 1800s, however, the arrival of steam propulsion caused a dramatic change in ship design. Ships needed to become more streamlined in order to cope with the increase in speed now provided by steam.

The early steamships were propelled by large paddle wheels, but by the mid-1800s propellers proved to be more efficient. However, steam engines were often unreliable and steam did not replace sail immediately. Many steamships were equipped with sails in case their engines broke down. The great clippers that sailed between America, China, Australia and Britain in the

Right: SMS *Rheinland* was a World War I German battleship. She had 29-cm-thick armour plating, 12 28-cm guns, 12 15-cm guns and 16 8·6-cm guns. Her top speed was 39 km/hour and her displacement 19,200 tonnes.

Wireless aerials
Lookouts
Searchlights
Navigating bridge
Gun turret
28-cm gun
Anchor
Crane for lifting out boats
Secondary armament, 15-cm guns
Secondary armament, 8·6-cm guns
Armour plating

---

in Washington and agreed that all the world's maps should be drawn with the prime meridian at Greenwich. The French and Brazilians did not immediately agree, only changing their maps in 1911.

Q **Quadrant** was an instrument used in the 1500s to 1700s to measure the angle between the Pole Star and the horizon. It consisted of a quarter circle of wood with a scale marked 0° to 90° along its curved edge. A weighted line hung from the right-angled corner. The Pole Star was sighted through 2 holes along 1 straight edge and the angle of the star was indicated by the line on the scale.

Quinquireme, *see* BIREME.

R **Radar** (*Radio detection and ranging*) uses radio waves to detect the position of objects. A rotating scanner emits a stream of radio-wave pulses. When these strike an object they are reflected back and picked up by the same scanner. Pulses from nearby objects return to the scanner more quickly than those from distant objects and the information is transferred electronically to a round screen, similar to that of a television. A dot in the middle of the screen indicates the ship's position and a bright radius sweeps round the screen at the same rate as the scanner. Objects appear as bright dots or areas on the screen, which is marked with a distance scale. Radar can also be used to detect the speed of objects using the DOPPLER EFFECT.

Royal Observatory at Greenwich, London, was founded by Charles II. He made the English astronomer John Flamsteed the first Astronomer Royal with the task of cataloguing the stars in order to help improve navigation. Thanks to the recent invention of the telescope Flamsteed was able to catalogue a large number of stars and compiled the first great star map of the age. He also observed the movements of the Moon and predicted the times of tides. The Royal Observatory is now in East Sussex.

S **Sacred calabash** was a navigation instrument

Radar scanner

Across the Oceans

Below: 1. *Ark Royal*, the famous British aircraft carrier, was launched in 1950. She was refitted after 20 years and finally ended service in 1978.
2. The 2,330-tonne *Glückauf* was the world's first tanker. Ordered by Germany, she was built in Scotland in 1893.
3. A German IX-92 World War II U-boat, which carried 12 torpedoes and could travel at about 35 km/hour on the surface.
4. The 84,771-tonne *Normandie* was a French liner launched in 1932. She had turbo-electric power capable of producing 160,000 hp.

mid- to late 1800s were fast, sleek sailing ships that did not use steam at all.

As steam power became more reliable and coal and oil became cheaper, steamships replaced sailing ships for carrying cargo and passengers. Only on the really long-haul voyages were sailing ships still needed, as they did not have to stop at frequent intervals to take on coal. But by the early 1900s more efficient steam engines, particularly the steam turbine, ensured the supremacy of the steamship.

Wooden ships too became obsolete. Iron ships were more durable and in warships armour plate was needed against the new exploding shells that were being used. In the early 1900s there was a rapid growth in the construction of fighting ships as Europe prepared for World War I. Sleek, fast-moving battleships, cruisers and destroyers appeared. And the Germans developed the first practical submarines, which were powered by internal combustion engines (*see page 18*) on the surface and by electric batteries underwater.

Since then ships have changed little in basic shape. However, new materials, techniques and ideas have led to changes in the design of various parts, such as hulls and bows. Many ships are now powered by diesel engines and the installation of nuclear-powered engines in some ships has enabled them to avoid the need for refuelling. Ships have also taken on specialized roles. For example, car ferries, aircraft carriers, giant tankers, container ships and ice-breakers are all designed to do their particular jobs.

Modern navigation

Although aeroplanes have taken much cargo and many passengers from the sea, the increasing amount of trade and tourism round the world has led to an ever-growing volume of traffic across the oceans. As a result it is more important than ever for a navigator to know not only where he is, but also what hazards, such as rocks and other ships, are nearby.

The introduction of radio into ships has changed both communications and navigation. Instead of having to rely on flag and light signals, ships can now communicate with each other and with the shore without necessarily being in sight. In 1910 Ethel Le Neve and Harvey Crippen, who had poisoned his wife, were arrested on board ship in the Atlantic Ocean as a result of early radio communications.

The first radio direction-finding (RDF) system used in navigation was the D/F loop. This used a loop aerial which could be rotated until the signal from a shore-based transmitting station faded out completely. The loop was then at exactly 90° to the direction of the signal. By taking the bearings of two such signals the ship's position could be plotted on a chart. Today, RDF systems automatically indicate the ship's position on an instrument.

The modern DECCA, DECTRA and LORAN systems are considerably more accurate. They work on the principle that two signals transmitted simultaneously from stations at equal distances from a ship will arrive at the same moment. If the ship is nearer one station than the other, the signal from the first station will arrive a fraction of a second before the signal from the second station. The distances from the stations can then be calculated electronically and the ship's position can then be found.

Another instrument that has revolutionized

used by the natives of Hawaii. It consisted of a gourd hollowed-out into a bowl. A notch was cut in the rim and, opposite this at a certain distance below the rim, a sighting hole was drilled. Below this hole the gourd was drilled with a ring of holes. These ensured that the calabash was held level when filled with water. When the Pole Star could be sighted through the hole and the notch the navigator knew that he was on the same latitude as Hawaii.
Sextant is the modern instrument for finding LATITUDE by measuring the angle between the Sun or a star and the horizon. The arm of the instrument is moved so that the image of the star reflected by the index mirror and the half-silvered horizon mirror appears to rest on the horizon. The angle of the star can then be read from the scale. If it is turned on its side the instrument can also be used to measure angles between objects on the Earth's surface. The arm can be moved through an angle of 60° and this allows angles of up to 120° to be measured.

Ship-of-the-line was the name given to the largest type of sailing warship. The name is derived from the way in which naval battles were fought in the 1700s and 1800s. Two opposing fleets formed up in lines alongside each other and tried to pound each other to pieces with cannon.
Sonar (*So*und *n*avigation *a*nd *r*anging) is a method of detecting underwater objects using sound waves. A transducer emits pulses of ultrasonic (very high frequency) waves, which are reflected from the sea bed or

British ship-of-the-line (left) and frigate (right), 1800s

Universe Ireland 1968

navigation is the gyroscope. A GYROCOMPASS always points towards True North and can assist the navigator greatly when he sets the ship's course. An INERTIAL GUIDANCE SYSTEM also uses gyroscopes to work out the ship's position. It works on the same dead reckoning system used by Columbus, except that it is far more accurate.

To avoid rocks, sandbanks and other vessels, ships can use two other electrical navigation aids: SONAR and RADAR. Sonar equipment emits pulses of ultrasound (very high frequency sound, inaudible to the human ear) and picks up the echoes reflected by underwater objects. In an echo-sounder a trace records the depth of water beneath the ship. In ASDIC, one of the earliest forms of sonar, the pulses and echoes are converted into audible sound in the form of 'pings' to detect the presence and movement of submarines. Radar uses radio waves to detect nearby ships and land in the same way as an echo-sounder uses sound waves. The radio waves reflected from an object are used to form a pattern on a screen, rather like a television screen, on which ships appear as bright dots.

Electrical aids alone, however, are not enough and navigators must learn many of the traditional methods of navigation. Knowledge of the rules of the sea, of how to take compass bearings and of how to use a chart are still important, particularly in crowded coastal waters. The chronometer and sextant are still essential instruments, especially in smaller boats. Lighthouses, first used in Egypt in 280 BC, and lightships are needed to mark dangerous rocks. Systems of buoys are required to mark safe channels, wrecks and sandbanks. Therefore the art of the navigator should not be allowed to die. The all too frequent collisions and wrecks that cause severe oil pollution of our seas and shores show what can result from lack of navigational skill.

Above: The supertanker *Universe Ireland* is over 300 metres long and 53 metres wide. Built in 1968, she has two steam turbines and can produce 37,400 hp.

Below: Sonar equipment emits high-frequency sound impulses and from the reflected echoes can detect the depth of water underneath the ship, or the direction, range and speed of a submarine.

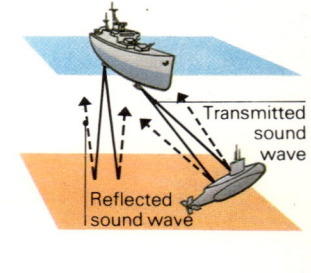

Left: A diesel engined patrol submarine which is capable of high underwater speeds and can maintain continuous submerged patrols. It is equipped to fire homing torpedoes.

underwater object and picked up by a receiver. *See also* ASDIC.

Square-rigged ships were those in which the principal sails were square and slung crosswise on horizontal booms attached to the masts. *See also* FORE-AND-AFT.

Starboard is the right-hand side of a ship. The Viking ships had their steering oars on this side and the term literally means 'steering side' of the ship. *See also* PORT.

T Traverse board was a navigation aid used in the 1400s. Sailors could not read or write, so at half-hourly intervals they used the pegs on a traverse board to record the direction of the wind and the approximate speed of the ship. The pilot could later use this information to estimate the progress and position of the ship.

Trireme, *see* BIREME.

Twig charts were used by the Polynesians. The twigs were bound together with fibre and islands were marked with cowrie shells tied to the twigs. Long, straight twigs indicated the directions of islands; curved twigs showed how wave directions were altered by islands; and short, straight twigs indicated currents.

V Variation is the difference in degrees between True North and the direction in which a compass needle points. This difference is due to the fact that the Earth's magnetic poles are situated some distance from the geographical poles. Thus magnetic variation is different in different parts of the world. It also changes slightly from year to year, as the magnetic poles are gradually changing position.

Z Zenith is the point in the sky directly above an observer. The zenith distance is the angle between the Sun and the zenith. *See also* DECLINATION.

Square-rigged ship

Traverse board

In developed countries, a car is regarded by many families not as a luxury but as a necessity. Yet the technology of mass production, which made cars cheap to buy, was introduced only in the first decade of this century.

Travelling by Road

As the villages, towns and cities of early civilizations grew, so the trading routes between them also grew in importance. Paths, along which men travelled on horseback, developed into roads where carts and wagons could travel. For over 5,000 years horse-drawn chariots, carriages and coaches remained the most efficient means of transport. However, in the 1700s and 1800s the Industrial Revolution gave rise to a series of inventions that led to mechanized transport and, gradually, horse-drawn carriages became obsolete.

The invention of steam power caught the imagination of many people. The first practical steam road vehicle was a gun-tractor built by the French engineer N. J. Cugnot in 1769 and used by the French army. Several inventors also attempted to produce commercially-successful steam cars. Richard Trevithick (*see page 47*), for example, built a series of them between 1801 and 1811. His 'London Carriage' proved its worth by trundling slowly along Oxford Street in London in 1802. But Trevithick could not persuade anyone to take much interest in them so he turned his attention to the railways. By 1840 steam coaches had almost disappeared from the roads. There were probably two main reasons for this. First, they were frightening vehicles, inclined to belch smoke and sparks, and many people expected them to explode. Second, and probably more important, the rich and influential businessmen who owned the fleets of horsedrawn carriages, saw that steam coaches could upset their trade and so caused trouble for anyone operating them. A law was passed prohibiting the use of horseless vehicles unless a man walked in front carrying a red flag. The speed limit for such vehicles was set at 6 km/hour in the country and 3 km/hour in towns.

At the same time as people were trying out steam power, other experiments using mechanized transport were being devised. In 1826 Sam Brown, an English engineer, built a mechanical carriage that progressed with a series of loud bangs. Inside the CYLINDERS, which were similar to those of a steam engine, a series of gas explosions drove the PISTONS. After years of experimenting, a German engineer called Nikolaus Otto set up a factory to build gas engines. His production manager was Gottlieb Daimler (1834–1900). Otto devised a four-stroke cycle for his engines and they were a great success.

Meanwhile, an Austrian engineer, Siegfried Marcus, was working out ways to develop the use of petrol as a fuel. He used this portable, easily-vaporized liquid in several engines that he built between 1864 and 1874. But the first major advance was made by Daimler. In 1885 he devised the first high-speed, single-cylinder, petrol-driven engine. He tried this out first on a three-wheeled tricycle and afterwards on a four-wheeled car in 1886.

At the same time Karl Benz (1844–1929), another German engineer, was also producing successful engines, unknown to Daimler. While Daimler's main interest was in building engines, Benz saw the commercial possibilities in motor cars. In 1885 he built his first car, a three-

Below: Cugnot's steam tractor (1769) was the first self-propelled vehicle. It was intended for hauling field guns. However, it had two main disadvantages. The boiler was not strong enough to withstand high pressures and so tended to run out of steam very quickly. Also, the heavy boiler was supported in the front axle and this made steering difficult.

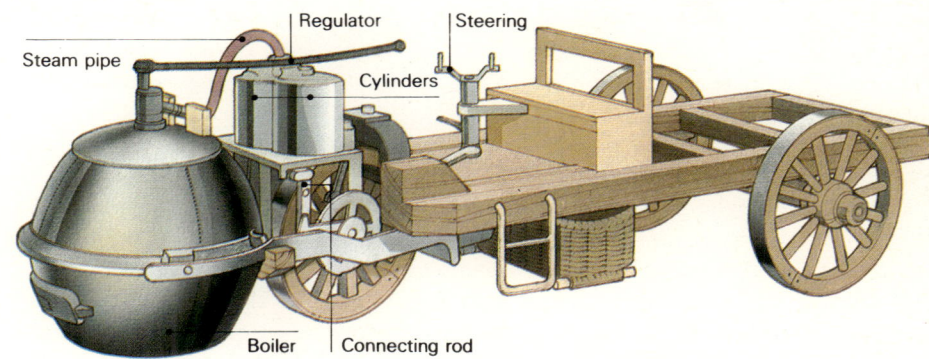

Reference

Accelerator is the pedal used to control the speed of a car. It is linked to the throttle in the CARBURETTOR by a cable, rod or air tube.
Air-cooled engines are cooled by air which may be blown through ducts by a fan. Such engines have fins on the CYLINDER block to help remove the heat.
Alternator, see GENERATOR.
Antifreeze is a mixture of chemicals added to the water in the cooling system to stop it freezing. The main constituent is ethylene glycol, an alcohol, which reduces the freezing point of water. Anti-corrosion agents are also added to the mixture.
Austin 7 was also known as the 'Baby Austin'. Over 250,000 were sold between 1922 and 1938. 4-cylinder, 747-cc, side-valve engine; top speed 72 km/hour.
Automatic transmission uses an automatic CLUTCH and an EPICYCLIC GEAR SYSTEM to keep the engine speed (roughly) constant.

Battery (more correctly called an accumulator) contains a series of electrical cells, each of which has an output of 2 volts. Each cell consists of 2 lead-compound plates immersed in sulphuric acid. Charging the battery causes chemical changes to take place in the plates. The chemical changes are reversed when the battery discharges.
Bayonne Bridge has the second longest steel arch span in the world (503.5 metres). It bridges the Kill Van Kull between Staten Island, New York, and Bayonne, New Jersey.
Bearing is a device that supports a fixed part on a rotating wheel or shaft and reduces the friction between them. Ball bearings use steel balls between an inner race (fixed to the stationary part) and an outer race (fixed to the rotating part). Roller

Austin 7

Bayonne Bridge

18 Travelling by Road

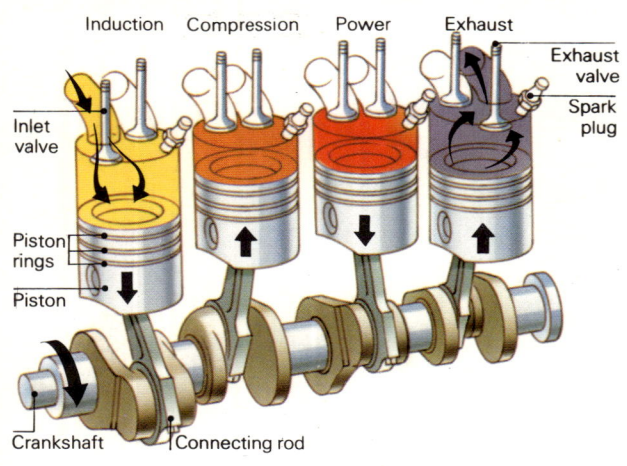

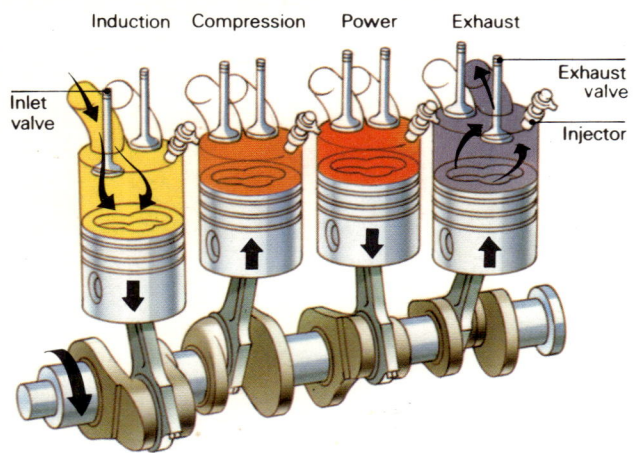

Far left: A four-cylinder petrol engine.

Left: The same four-stroke cycle occurs in a diesel engine. However, only air is drawn in during the induction stroke. During the compression stroke the air becomes hot and when fuel is injected into the combustion chamber it ignites spontaneously, resulting in the power stroke.

Below: A Bardon motor car in about 1900. Bardons were built from 1899 to 1903. The first model had a 2,000 cc, 4–5 hp engine mounted under the floor. The engine had a single cylinder that contained 2 opposed pistons. The final drive consisted of a double chain. The 1901 model had 2 cylinders mounted under the bonnet. The 1902 model had a shaft drive instead of the chain drive.

wheeler with a tubular steel chassis. It had a 0.5 horsepower engine and could reach about 15 km/hour. Three years later Benz became the first man to offer cars for sale to the public.

Internal combustion engines

Nikolaus Otto's four-stroke engine cycle was originally designed for use in a gas engine. However, Otto's work led the way towards petrol engines and today most cars, motor bikes, buses and lorries are propelled by engines that have four-stroke cycles. This cycle is so called because only one stroke in four produces power. The other three strokes are concerned with drawing in the fuel (induction), compressing it (compression) and letting out the exhaust gases (exhaust).

In a petrol engine the induction stroke begins as the piston inside the cylinder moves down. This occurs as a result of the turning movement of the CRANKSHAFT. At the same time the inlet VALVE at the top of the cylinder opens and a mixture of air and petrol vapour is drawn in. During the compression stroke the piston moves upwards again, the inlet valve closes and the air and petrol are compressed into a small space. Near the end of the compression stroke the gases are ignited by a spark from the SPARK PLUG. They burn explosively and the gases that are produced as they burn, expand rapidly. Thus the piston is forced downwards. This power stroke causes the crankshaft to continue turning. When the power stroke has ended, the piston once again moves upwards. At the same time the exhaust valve opens and the waste gases are expelled. At the end of the exhaust stroke the piston is ready to begin the next induction stroke.

In practice an engine usually has more than one cylinder and each cylinder fires in turn. Thus in a four-cylinder engine, the type commonly used in cars, when the first piston is performing its induction stroke, the second piston is on its compression stroke, the third is on its power stroke and the last is on its exhaust stroke. For smooth running of the engine the cylinders do not fire in the order one, two, three, four (one is at the front of the engine). In most British cars the firing order is one, three, four, two.

In 1890, a few years after Benz and Daimler had begun producing their petrol engines, Herbert Stuart, a British engineer, patented the first compression-ignition engine. In 1893 a German engineer, Rudolf Diesel (1858–1913), produced a better version which he perfected in 1897. This type of engine has since been known as the diesel engine. It has a four-stroke cycle and works in much the same way as the petrol engine. However, the fuel is ignited in a different way. During the induction stroke only air is drawn into the cylinder. During the compression stroke the compression ratio (the amount by which the air is compressed) is high, much higher than in a petrol engine, and as a result the air gets very hot. At the top of the compression stroke both valves are closed and fuel is injected into the cylinder. It immediately ignites in the hot air, causing the power stroke, which is followed by the exhaust stroke.

The advantage of a diesel engine is that it can run on cheaper fuel than petrol. Diesel fuel has a higher flash point (the temperature at which it

---

bearings use steel rollers instead of balls. A bush bearing consists of a replaceable soft metal alloy sleeve in between the moving parts. A shell bearing is a sleeve bearing composed of 2 halves (*see also* BIG END).
Benz Velo was the first car to go into quantity production, as a 3-wheeler in 1886 and as a 4-wheeler from 1892 to 1901. Single-cylinder (2-cylinder from 1897), horizontally-mounted 2,540-cc engine; top speed 25 km/hour.
Big end is the larger end of the piston rod, a connecting rod, joined to the crankshaft by a shell bearing. Knocking of the big end is due to failure of the bearing, caused by lack of oil.

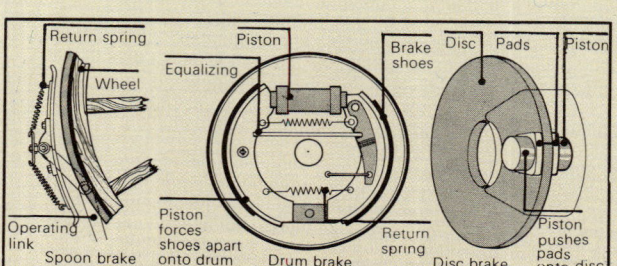

Types of brakes

Brakes are the means by which a moving vehicle can be stopped. Usually, drum brakes or disc brakes, both operated by a hydraulic system, are used and act on all 4 wheels.

C Camber of a road is the slightly rounded shape of the surface. It allows water to drain away.
Camshaft is a shaft on which cams (unevenly distributed projections) are carried. Thus, as the shaft rotates, a rod touching a cam is made to move up and down. The camshaft operates the VALVES, DISTRIBUTOR and oil pump. In many engines it is situated within the cylinder block, but some engines have one or two over- head camshafts situated under the rocker cover at the top of the engine.
Capacity is the total volume of fuel mixture drawn into an engine during a complete cycle as the pistons each move from top to bottom of their cylinders, i.e. the total volume of an engine's cylinders excluding the combustion chambers. It is measured in litres (l) or cubic centimetres (cc).
Carburettor is the device used to supply the engine with the correct mixture of air and vaporized petrol. It operates by engine suction

Travelling by Road

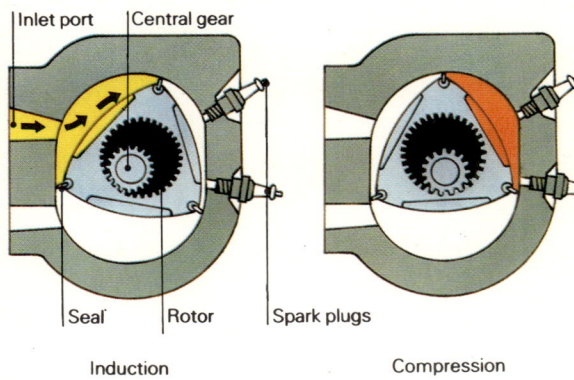
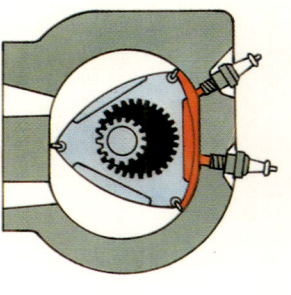
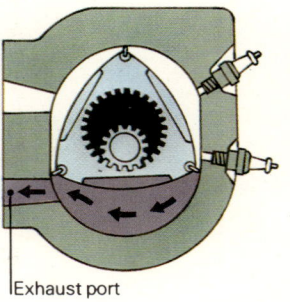

Induction — Compression — Power — Exhaust

Left: In a Wankel engine the rotor takes over the function of the pistons. As it moves round, fuel and air are drawn in through the inlet port. When the trailing seal has passed the inlet port, compression begins. When fully compressed, the mixture is ignited by spark plugs. The resulting power 'stroke' forces the rotor to continue turning. Exhaust gases leave through the exhaust port.

and the amount of fuel entering the engine is controlled by a butterfly valve called the throttle. Petrol from the petrol tank is pumped into a reservoir called the float chamber, which maintains a constant pressure supply to the carburettor. Inside a carburettor there are 1 or more jets, small holes through which the petrol is vaporized. A fixed jet carburettor has a main jet, used for constant high-speed running, and 2 or more other jets to allow the engine to idle or accelerate rapidly. A variable jet carburettor has only 1 jet. When the throttle is opened the increased suction from the engine causes a needle to be pulled out of the jet, allowing more petrol through. *See also* CHOKE.

Choke is a device in a CARBURETTOR for increasing the ratio of petrol to air in the mixture that enters the engine, either by reducing the amount of air or by increasing the amount of petrol. Choke, or venturi, is also the name given to the narrowing of the air passage in a carburettor where the air passes over the jet. This narrowing causes the speed of the air to increase, which results in a lowering of the air pressure and petrol is sucked into the air-stream.

Clutch is a device for controlling the engagement of the engine drive with the gearbox. In a single-plate clutch the friction plate is forced against the engine FLYWHEEL by several springs. In a diaphragm clutch the springs are replaced by a single diaphragm spring. There are also several kinds of automatic clutch. The type commonly used in AUTOMATIC TRANSMISSION systems is a fluid-coupling called a torque converter.

Coil is the electrical device in a car used to create high voltage (high tension) current. Low voltage current flows from the battery to a primary coil. The current passes through 2 contact breaker points in the DISTRIBUTOR. As the rotor arm of the distributor rotates the points open and close to interrupt the flow of current. The build up and fall of low voltage current in the primary coil induces pulses of high voltage current in an inner secondary coil.

Compression ratio is the ratio of the volume of fuel mixture when the piston is at the end of its induction

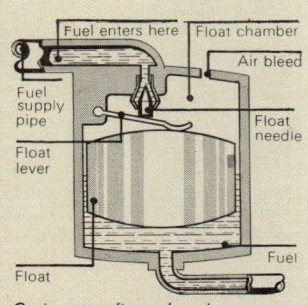
Carburettor float chamber

Left: 1. A Benz Velo of 1885, the year before it went into quantity production. The drive was by means of chains and belts to the rear axle.
2. A 1911 Austin 18/24. It could produce 45 hp and had a top speed of 80 km/hour.
3. A 1913 Fiat 508 Balilla coupé. It had a 990-cc engine and could produce 22 hp. All four wheels were fitted with hydraulic brakes.
4. A 1945 Volkswagen Beetle, which later became one of the most popular cars in the world.
5. A 24-hp Wolseley London General Bus of 1908.

will ignite) than petrol and is therefore safer to use. However, it also freezes more readily than petrol and thus can cause problems in very cold weather. In addition, diesel engines are heavy and generally less suitable for cars than for heavy transport, such as lorries and diesel-electric railway engines.

Petrol and diesel piston-engines are still very much in use today. But during the 1950s Dr Felix Wankel, a German engineer, developed an entirely new kind of petrol engine. The Wankel engine does not have pistons. Instead, a rotor shaped like a triangle with curved sides revolves inside a combustion chamber. The rotor turns on a smaller rotating central GEAR that forms part of the crankshaft. It rotates around the chamber and the gap between each side of the rotor and the wall of the chamber expands and contracts and causes the four-stroke cycle. The engine has no valves; fuel is drawn in and the waste gases are expelled automatically through open inlet and exhaust ports.

The full cycle can be shown by following one side of the rotor through one complete revolution. As it comes opposite the inlet port the space between it and the wall expands and the fuel and air mixture is drawn in (induction). As the rotor moves round, the space contracts and the mixture is compressed (compression). When this is complete the mixture is ignited by a spark plug and the resulting expansion of the burning gases

Right: 6. A 1930 Mack Model AC articulated lorry. The driving axle had solid rubber tyres, although the front wheels and those of the trailer had pneumatic tyres.

stroke to the volume when the piston is at the end of its compression stroke. In modern petrol-engined cars the ratio is about 8:1 or 9:1. Diesel engines have compression ratios of between 12:1 and 25:1.
Crankshaft is the shaft that, through connecting rods, converts the up-and-down motion of the pistons into a rotary action.
Crown wheel and pinion are two bevel GEARS which transmit the rotation of the propeller shaft to the DIFFERENTIAL. The pinion is the driving gear at the end of the propeller shaft and the crown wheel is fixed to the cage of the differential.
Cylinder is a tubular space in the engine block in which gases from the carburettor are ignited, so forcing the piston down to drive the engine. Most cars have 4 cylinders and their total CAPACITY is given as the engine size.

D **Derailleur gear** on a modern bicycle consists of several different sizes of SPROCKET on which the chain can run. The mechanism lifts the chain from one sprocket to another and a tensioning device takes up slack as the chain moves from a larger to a smaller sprocket.

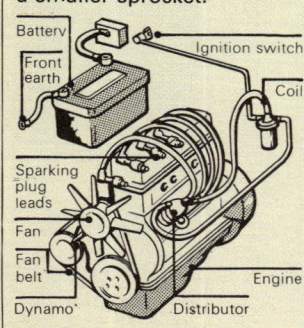

Distributor in ignition system

Differential is an assembly of 4 bevel GEARS that allows the driven wheels of a car to rotate at different speeds when the car turns a corner.
Distributor is the device, operated by a gear on the camshaft, that distributes the high voltage current from the COIL to the SPARK PLUGS. The rotor arm is permanently connected to the high tension lead from the coil. As it rotates, it passes on the pulses of high voltage current to each distributor terminal in succession. This causes each spark plug to produce a spark. On the distributor shaft there are raised cams (1 for each spark plug) which push against a contact breaker arm, forcing the contact breaker points apart. After each cam has passed a spring presses the points together.
Draisienne was a 2-wheeled hobby horse made in 1818. Its front wheel was steerable and it could be made to reach 16 km/hour.
Dynamo, see GENERATOR.

E **Epicyclic gear systems** are used in bicycles and in cars with automatic transmission. This

keeps the rotor turning (power). When the mixture is fully burned, the space begins to decrease and the waste gases are expelled (exhaust).

The motor car through the years

Although Daimler and Benz did not invent the motor car, they did make it into a viable commercial proposition. Two brilliant engineers, they brought together a number of inventions and improved on them so that the modern car evolved from their efforts. After Benz, many other manufacturers opened up, including such famous names as Panhard and Levassor, Renault, Peugeot, Austin, Morris and Ford.

Rene Panhard (1841–1908) and Emile Levassor were building cars with engines underneath in 1889. But by 1891 they were producing cars with engines at the front, which kept them clear of road dirt and helped improve the cars' balance. They also used sliding pinion gears for changing speed. These were a great improvement on the belts and pulleys used by Benz as more power could be transferred to the wheels.

Independent suspension was already in use, having been introduced in 1873 on a steam carriage. The CARBURETTOR was invented in 1884 and the modern float-type carburettor was first used in 1892. The steering wheel, which replaced the steering lever, or tiller, was first introduced in 1894 (*see* STEERING SYSTEM). In 1895 the Michelin brothers in France began producing pneumatic (air-filled) TYRES, which had been invented in 1888 by a Scottish vet called John Dunlop (1840–1921).

The repeal of the 'red flag' law and the raising of the speed limit in 1896 to 22.5 km/hour, provided further incentive for improving parts of the car. By 1899 multi-cylinder engines had appeared, together with the honeycomb RADIATOR and SHAFT DRIVE, which gradually replaced the chain drive used on most early cars. Daimler had introduced the floor-mounted ACCELERATOR and Renault had adopted the UNIVERSAL JOINT used on modern cars.

As the speed of cars increased, so braking efficiency also had to improve. The first cars used wooden blocks applied to the rear wheels. In 1902 Renault fitted drum BRAKES to his cars and in the same year Frederick Lanchester (1868–1946), a British car manufacturer, invented the disc brake. However, this did not become widely accepted until the late 1950s.

During the early 1900s the motor car industry was expanding very rapidly, particularly in America. Many parts of the modern motor car date from this period, including AUTOMATIC TRANSMISSION, the DISTRIBUTOR, electric starting and lighting, the DYNAMO and hydraulic braking.

Until about 1915 comfortable cars were an expensive luxury. In 1903, however, the Cadillac and Oldsmobile companies in America introduced a new principle — cars with interchangeable parts. This was the first step towards mass-production. Henry Ford took up this idea and in 1908 began manufacturing the now famous FORD MODEL T. By 1927, when the factory making this model closed down, 15 million of these cars had been produced. This was the world's first mass-produced basic car. Because it was cheap and easy to run and maintain, it proved to be an immensely popular car.

After World War I manufacturers found themselves with markets for both luxury and mass-produced cars. Those who could afford them wanted the best models and many high-quality cars were built to a fine standard of craftsmanship. Such cars as the Bugatti-Royale Type 41 and Hispano-Suiza H6B were probably among the finest cars ever built. Unfortunately, the combination of the American Depression in the 1930s and competition with mass-produced

Below: The Ford Model T was popular in America and all over Europe. This 1909 version comes from a museum in Portugal. Henry Ford (1863–1947) built his first motor car in 1893 and in 1908 he thought up the idea of manufacturing cars on an assembly line. Using this system, together with interchangeable parts, he set out to build a car that was cheap and reliable. The success of the Model T paved the way for all later mass-produced cars.

---

type of system uses 2 or 4 small pinions (planetary GEARS) mounted on a carrier. These revolve round a central sun gear and mesh with an outer ring called the annulus. A car that has AUTOMATIC TRANSMISSION uses 2 or more sets of epicyclic gears. The input drive is transmitted to the first annulus and the output is driven by the last annulus. Changing gear is achieved by using band brakes and clutches automatically applied to certain parts of the system at appropriate speeds. A bicycle has 2 sets of 4 planets, 2 sun gears and a single annulus. Changing gear is achieved by moving the sun gears horizontally so that they mesh with different parts of the system.
Expressway, *see* MOTORWAY.

F **Flywheel** is a heavy wheel fixed to the rear end of the CRANKSHAFT. When the engine is running the momentum of the flywheel keeps the crankshaft turning smoothly in between individual power strokes. The rim of the flywheel has gear teeth which mesh with the STARTER MOTOR pinion when the engine is being started.
Ford Model T, also known as the 'Tin Lizzie', was mass-produced by Henry Ford between 1908 and 1927. 4-cylinder, 2,898-cc engine; 2-speed (forward) EPICYCLIC gearbox (and a reverse gear), operated by pedals; top speed 64 km/hour.
Forth Road Bridge was the first major suspension bridge built in Britain (1958–64). It has a main span of 1,006 metres, the longest in Britain, and side spans of 408 metres. It is the northernmost (latitude 56°N) major bridge in the world and high winds caused great problems during its erection.
Fuel injection is used on some cars instead of a CARBURETTOR. A measured amount of fuel is pumped through a fine nozzle into the inlet port of each cylinder at the beginning of the induction stroke.

G **Gears** are toothed wheels mostly used to transmit movement from one rotating shaft to another. Simple spur gears

Forth Road Bridge

Travelling by Road

cars, caused many of the custom-built car firms to go out of business. Only a few manufacturers of high-quality cars, such as Lancia and Rolls Royce, survive from this era.

Many firms that produced cheaper cars also went out of business as a result of the intense competition. Two of the most successful cars in Europe in the 1920s were the AUSTIN 7, or Baby Austin, and the MORRIS COWLEY. One advantage was their low horsepower. Thus in 1921 when car tax was raised to £1 per horsepower they became cheaper to run than the Ford Model T.

Over the years car design continued to improve and many innovations were added as manufacturers vied with each other for a share of the ever-increasing market. One of the great testing-grounds for cars was the race track. Many standard items on modern cars began life on a racing car, including detachable wheels (which allowed spare wheels to be carried) and radial tyres. Streamlining, too, was first introduced into racing cars, but found its way into the popular car market as the family cars of the 1930s reached higher speeds. Improvements in fuel systems and engine technology led to lighter, more powerful engines and the resulting increase in power-to-weight ratio caused improvements to acceleration, speed, road-holding and braking.

In addition to cars other vehicles were now being constructed. The first lorry was built by Daimler in 1896 and by 1910 there were vans, trucks, lorries and fire-engines on the road. Until

Right: 1. A Draisienne hobby horse of 1819. It had a steerable front wheel, an arm rest and a saddle. This type of hobby horse became very popular.
2. A Matchless Ordinary penny farthing bicycle of 1883.
3. A Starley Rover of 1888. It had solid rubber tyres and no brakes.
4. An 1894 Hildebrand and Wolfmüller motor cycle. Its two horizontal cylinders drove the rear wheels directly and it had a top speed of about 45 km/hour — faster than any car of the time.
5. A modern Lambretta, one of the most popular makes of motor scooter.

Right: 6. A 1925 Harley-Davidson 7/9 hp motor cycle with a sidecar attached.

---

have teeth set at the same angle as the shaft; in helical gears the teeth are set at an angle. If 2 different sized gears mesh together, the larger is called the gear and it rotates more slowly than the smaller, which is called the pinion. A bevel gear is shaped like the bottom half of a cone. Bevel gears are used to change not only the speed but also the axis of rotation.
Generator, or dynamo, is an engine-driven device that produces an electric current. The term dynamo is sometimes used to mean the D.C. generator of a car, which produces direct current (current flowing in one direction only). An A.C. generator, or alternator, produces an alternating current. It is simpler and more reliable than a D.C. generator and can charge the battery when the engine is idling.
Gladesville Bridge, across the Parramatta River, Sydney, Australia, is the world's longest-span reinforced concrete arch bridge. Completed in 1964, its main span is 304.8 metres long.
Golden Gate Suspension Bridge, built between 1933 and 1937 had, until 1964 (see VERRAZANO NARROWS BRIDGE), the longest span in the world (1,280 metres). It links the 2 sides of the entrance to San Francisco Bay Harbour.

H **Handbrake** is a device used to operate the rear brakes by means of cables and/or rods.
Horsepower (hp) is a unit of power used to describe the power output of an engine (1 hp = 550 ft-lb per sec; 1 ft-lb is the amount of work done by lifting a 1 lb weight through a vertical distance of 1 ft). This can be calculated from the work done by the pistons. However, some of this power is used up in overcoming friction in the engine. The proportion of power that remains can be measured by applying a brake (in an instrument called a dynamometer) to the drive shaft and is known as the brake horsepower (bhp).
Humber bicycle, first made in 1890, was the first to have the true diamond-shaped frame that, until the cross-frame became popular in the 1960s, was standard on all bicycles.

Golden Gate Bridge

the 1920s they ran on petrol and had solid rubber tyres. But diesel engines were more economical and pneumatic (air-filled) tyres were becoming more reliable and by the early 1930s most lorries were similar to those of today.

Horse-drawn buses were replaced in the mid-1800s by horse-drawn trams, which ran on rails set into the road. Steam trams were tried in the late 1800s, but were not a great success. Two other methods of replacing the horse were found. One was the cable car, which was a tram hauled along by a cable set into a groove in the road. San Francisco's cable cars, first devised in 1873, are still in use. The other method was the use of electricity. Batteries could not produce sufficient power for trams, so various forms of overhead cable were tried. In 1888 Frank Sprague, an American, devised a swivel trolley pole that was attached to the roof of the tramcar and ran underneath the cable. This system was later used in tramways all over the world.

Electric cars are generally thought of as a modern idea, but the first electric carriage was in fact built in 1837 by Robert Davidson, a Scottish engineer. Electric buses appeared in Paris (1881) and London (1888) and in 1897 London's first taxi cabs were powered by batteries. They could travel at 14 km/hour and had a range of 48 kilometres. In 1899 Camille Jenatzy, a Belgian, achieved 106 km/hour, breaking the land speed record of the time, in his bullet-shaped electric car called *La Jamais Contente*.

Today, electric cars do not have the speed or range needed by most car drivers. Their use is limited to milk-floats and similar vehicles that do a lot of stopping and starting but do not travel great distances. However, more advanced electric cars and vans are being developed and some can reach 80 km/hour. The cleanness of such cars has great appeal in a world which is now conscious of how much pollution is caused by exhaust fumes from internal combustion engines.

Bicycles and motorcycles

While some people were trying to produce steam carriages another form of mechanical transport was catching on. In about 1800 there was a craze for two-wheeled 'hobby horses', which were built of wood and iron. They consisted of two wheels, one behind the other, joined by a bar which carried a seat. The rider straddled the bar and propelled the machine by 'walking' it along the road.

The craze soon died down, but a Scottish blacksmith, Kirkpatrick Macmillan (1813–78), followed up the idea and invented the first bicycle in 1839. It had a steerable front wheel carried on a forked rod. It was driven by pedals at the front which worked backwards and forwards driving rods and cranks attached to the rear wheel. In 1861 two brothers who owned a Paris pram factory produced a bicycle called the Michaux Velocipede. This had pedals that turned the front wheel, and as a result the wheel could only turn as fast as the rider pedalled. The immediate solution to the problem of increasing the speed of the bicycle was to increase the size of the front wheel. However, wooden wheels, with their heavy spokes and bone-shaking iron rims, were too heavy, so experiments began to develop SUSPENSION WHEELS. James Starley (1831–81), the manager of an English sewing machine factory, used suspension wheels on his famous

Above: Mike Hailwood negotiates a bend in the TT races on the Isle of Man. Motor cycle racing is a popular sport.

Left: Bicycles are used as a cheap and healthy form of transport by people all over the world, such as these Peking schoolchildren. The tricycle cart in the background is heavily laden.

Humber Estuary Suspension Bridge, started in 1972 and at present scheduled to be opened in mid-1979, will have the longest span in the world (1,410 metres).

K Knocking, or pinking, is a hammering sound heard in the engine. It is due to premature firing of the fuel and can be caused by using unsuitable fuel (*see* OCTANE RATING).

M Manifold is a pipe or chamber that has several openings. A multicylinder engine has two man- ifolds attached to the cylinder head. The inlet manifold consists of pipes or channels that carry fuel from the carburettor to the inlet ports. The exhaust manifold carries waste gases from the exhaust ports to the exhaust pipe.

Morris Cowley

Minor roads connect hamlets and villages with each other and with PRIMARY and SECONDARY ROADS. In some places minor roads may be little more than tracks with only thin base courses (road metal). A road without a base course is described as unmetalled.

Mont Blanc Tunnel, completed in 1962, is the longest road tunnel in the world (11.6 km). It is 9 metres high and has a single, 2-lane carriageway.

Morris Cowley, the most famous being the 'Bullnose Morris', was produced in thousands between the 2 World Wars. 4-cylinder, side-valve, 11.9-hp, 1,550-cc Hotchkiss engine; 3-speed gearbox; top speed 85 km/hour.

Motorway, or expressway, is a multiple-carriage TRUNK ROAD with 2 or more lanes in each carriageway. Vehicles can only gain access to a motorway via slip roads and there are no junctions except at the ends of the motorway.

Moulton bicycle was introduced in 1962 and its design has been copied, with modifications, many times since. Moultons have wheels of between 35 and 50 cm diameter, an F-shaped cross-frame with no high crossbar, and suspension — a coil spring at the front and a rubber shock-absorber at the rear. The height of the saddle and handlebars can be adjusted freely.

Moulton bicycle

Travelling by Road

Above: Stages on a car assembly line.
1. The underbody and superstructure are welded together and the doors, boot and bonnet are fitted.
2. The body is thoroughly washed and sanded and then sprayed with two coats of primer paint and three coats of top colour.
3. The trimmings and fittings, such as windows, bumpers, steering, wiring and lights, are added.
4. The body is lowered on to the engine and transmission.
5. The wheels are fitted, the suspension, steering and all other components are examined and checked and the car is test-driven on rollers.
6. The finished car is tested for water leaks. Finally it is given a short road test and is then ready to be sold.

Right: The Audi NSU Ro80 was one of the first cars to use a Wankel engine. Its 2-rotor, 995-cc engine gives it a maximum speed of 180 km/hour. The main advantages of a Wankel engine are its small size and smooth running. However, its high fuel consumption is a problem that has not yet been solved.

PENNY FARTHING BICYCLE, with its huge front wheel and tiny rear wheel. In early models of this bicycle the wheels were driven by pedals directly attached to the hub, but by 1885 there were versions with a form of chain drive and brakes on both wheels. Such bicycles were difficult and dangerous to ride so Starley also designed cumbersome three- and four-wheeled versions for the less adventurous riders.

Starley invented the type of suspension wheel in use today, with criss-crossing wires. In 1885 his nephew, J. K. Starley, designed the first safety bicycle, the Starley Rover. It resembled modern bicycles and its rear wheel was driven by a chain. However, its solid rubber tyres made it something of a bone-shaker.

Dunlop's pneumatic tyres made cycling more comfortable after 1888, but at first they had to be stuck and bandaged to the wheel rims. Removable tyres were invented in 1890. Later safety bicycles incorporated springing to help reduce the bumpiness of the ride still further. Today, bicycles have lightweight frames, gears and freewheeling devices.

The first motorcycle was a Michaux Velocipede fitted with a steam engine in 1869 and over the next 15 years various steam bicycles were produced, some of which could reach 96 km/hour. They were probably very uncomfortable and hot to ride.

During the late 1800s and early 1900s, however, petrol-engined pedal cycles (now called mopeds) appeared. Some of these were converted into two-seater tricars by fitting a chair in front or behind. The side-car appeared in 1904 and is still sometimes used to provide extra seating capacity.

By the beginning of World War I motorcycle design had progressed considerably, largely due to the popularity of racing. The frames had become heavier, the seats lower and the front forks were sprung to reduce road-shocks. Some machines even had gearboxes with two or three gears. Today motorcycles are built in various sizes, ranging from small 250-cc (*see* CAPACITY) models to powerful 1,000-cc racers.

Building cars

Before producing a new car a manufacturer spends a great deal of time and money on working out the design. A prototype is built and thoroughly tested. When everything is seen to work satisfactorily the car can be mass-produced.

Identical parts, such as body-panels, engines and wheels, are made and taken to a point on the assembly line. Each mechanic stays in one place and as the line moves forward he fits a particular part to every car as it passes him. Parts are added in a carefully devised sequence, beginning with the body and finishing with the wheels. At the end of the line each identical car is tested before being sent out to the customer.

N **New River Gorge Bridge**, West Virginia, USA, is the world's longest steel arch bridge. Completed in 1976, it has a main span of 518.2 metres.

O **Octane rating** of a petrol is a measure of its anti-knock properties. A sample of the petrol is tested in a special engine and compared with a mixture of iso-octane and heptane. The percentage of octane in the mixture comparable to the petrol gives the octane number. Petrol grades are sold according to minimum octane ratings. In Britain there are 4 grades: 2-star (minimum 90 octane), 3-star (minimum 94.96 octane), 4-star (minimum 97.99 octane) and 5-star (minimum 100 octane). In other parts of Europe only 2 grades are generally available; premium, which varies between 92 and 100 octane, and regular, which varies between 78 and 95 octane.

P **Pavement** of a road consists of the various layers laid down on the SUBGRADE. Flexible pavements have surfaces of fine stones bound together with asphalt or tar. Below this there is a base course of gravel, well compacted down and often bound together with similar bituminous material to that used in the surface. Below the base course a sub-base course of crushed rock rests on the subgrade. Rigid pavements have surfaces of portland cement, usually reinforced with steel bars, laid on to the sub-base course.

Paving with granite blocks, c.1840

Penny farthing bicycles had front wheels up to 127 cm in diameter and rear wheels of about 60 cm diameter. The frame consisted of a single curved tube from the top of the front wheel-fork to the top of the rear wheel-fork. The saddle was mounted on the frame near the handlebars.

Piston is a circular plunger that fits inside a CYLINDER. A modern engine piston is made of a light aluminium alloy. It has 3 grooves around the upper part. Two of these are for compression rings, which prevent gases

Travelling by Road

Left: Mass-produced cars are put together on an assembly line. Here, as the line moves forward, each Audi is having its body trim added before the engine, transmission and wheels are fitted.

Below: Some of the most expensive makes of modern car are still hand built without an assembly line. Here skilled mechanics are assembling Rolls Royces.

The moving assembly line was first used by Henry Ford to build the Model T and today nearly all cars are built by this mass-production method. It is the fastest and most economical method of building cars. The main problems are keeping each mechanic supplied with all the parts he needs, finding the optimum speed of the line and ensuring that sufficient time is given for each stage to be completed.

How a car works

The main systems of a motor car are the engine, cooling system, CLUTCH and GEARS, TRANSMISSION, suspension, STEERING, BRAKES, fuel, exhaust and electrical systems.

The modern car engine, although it works on the relatively simple four-stroke cycle, is a complex piece of machinery. The CYLINDERS in which the pistons move up and down form part of the cylinder block. The PISTONS are connected by piston rods to the CRANKSHAFT, which lies in the lower part of the cylinder block, known as the crankcase. The up-and-down movement of the piston rods causes the crankshaft to turn.

The cylinder head bolts on to the top of the cylinder block. It contains the combustion chambers, SPARK PLUGS and VALVES. The valves fit into the inlet and exhaust openings at the top of each cylinder. They are operated by a rotating CAMSHAFT, which is driven by a belt or chain connected to the crankshaft.

The engine needs to be kept lubricated with oil, otherwise the friction between the moving parts would cause them to overheat and seize up. Below the crankcase is a reservoir of oil called the sump. An oil pump, operated by the camshaft, pumps oil through narrow passages in the cylinder block, which feeds oil to where it is needed.

Many engines are cooled by water which is kept circulating through channels in the cylinder

---

from escaping from the combustion chamber, and 1 is for a scraper ring, which prevents oil from entering the chamber. The piston is connected to the small end of a connecting rod by a gudgeon pin, which lies horizontally inside the piston. The gudgeon pin may be free or fixed to the connecting rod. Other kinds of piston are used in the hydraulic systems of a car, such as the BRAKES.

Pont de Quebec, across the St Lawrence River in Canada, has the longest cantilever span in the world (549 metres). Work on this bridge began in 1899. After a major structural failure, a major accident and the loss of 87 lives the bridge was finally opened in 1917. Intended originally as a railway bridge, it now has a railway track and 2 carriageways running along its 987-metre length.

Primary roads connect towns and cities with each other and with TRUNK ROADS.

R Radiator is used to cool the water of an engine's cooling system. It is composed of very many thin channels and so has a large surface area from which heat is lost. Cooling is aided by a fan.

Pont de Quebec

S Sault Sainte Marie Bridge, Michigan, USA, is the world's largest bascule bridge (drawbridge). Built in 1941, its opening span is 102 metres.

Secondary roads lead from PRIMARY ROADS and link small towns and villages to each other.

Servo-assisted brakes use the vacuum created in the inlet manifold by suction from the engine. When the brake pedal is depressed, the small movement of fluid in the master cylinder operates an air valve. This allows air to pass to one side of a

block by an engine driven pump. Hoses connect these channels to a radiator fanned with air where the water is cooled before passing back into the system.

The rotating movement of the crankshaft is transferred to the wheels via the clutch, gearbox and transmission. The clutch is a device for connecting the engine to the gearbox. Most cars have a single-plate clutch. When the driver lifts his foot off the clutch pedal, a friction plate, which is connected to the gearbox, is forced by springs against the engine flywheel and both turn together.

The gearbox contains a number of toothed wheels, or gears, to transmit the engine power to the wheels. The engine produces the most power when running at high speed and the gears are used to slow down the speed of rotation so that the wheels need not turn so fast, particularly when the car is starting from rest. In a simple gearbox the gear lever is used to move two or more gears so that they interlock (mesh) and turn together. Changing gear with the early gearboxes could be a noisy and tiring business, but with the invention of synchromesh, gear-changing has become easier. Synchromesh is a device that synchronizes the speeds of two gearwheels, making sure that when they actually mesh they are rotating at the same speed.

In modern gearboxes all the gears are constantly in mesh. Gear-changing is achieved by moving two selector rings that revolve with the transmission shaft. Sliding one of these rings backwards or forwards causes it to engage a small dog gear attached to the required main gear. Today some cars have AUTOMATIC TRANSMISSION, a system which uses an automatic clutch and an arrangement of special gears to select the most appropriate gear ratio for the speed of the car.

The transmission system conveys the power to the wheels. In many rear-wheel drive cars the transmission shaft of the gearbox is connected by a UNIVERSAL JOINT to the propeller shaft. This type of joint allows the rotation to be transmitted while at the same time allowing the propeller shaft to move up and down. The rear end of the propeller shaft is connected to the final drive unit by another universal joint. The final drive unit

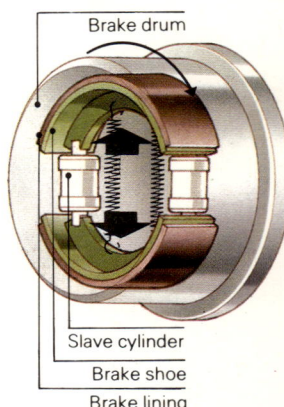

Above: In a drum brake an increase in brake fluid pressure in the slave cylinder forces the two brake shoes apart and the linings make contact with the inside of the drum.

Below right: A 'ghost' drawing of a Ford Fiesta Ghia 1100. Fiestas are a range of useful hatchback cars of which the Ghia is the most luxurious. The Ghia 1300 is the fastest, having a top speed of 158 km/hour. The Ghia 1100 has a top speed of 145 km/hour and its actual engine capacity is 1117 cc. Like the other Fiestas it has a 4-cylinder transverse engine and front wheel drive. Its braking system is servo-assisted and there are disc brakes on the front wheels and drum brakes on the rear wheels. The steering is rack and pinion and both front and rear suspensions include coil springs and telescopic dampers. On the Ghia 1300 there is an additional anti-roll bar at the rear.

Left: Safety is an increasingly important factor in modern car design and manufacturers use crash tests to find out how each part of a newly-designed car will behave in a collision. The front end of the car is designed to crumple on impact, so that some of the shock is absorbed. Other safety features that can be tried out in such tests include collapsible steering columns, safety windscreens, head rests and impact-absorbing bumpers.

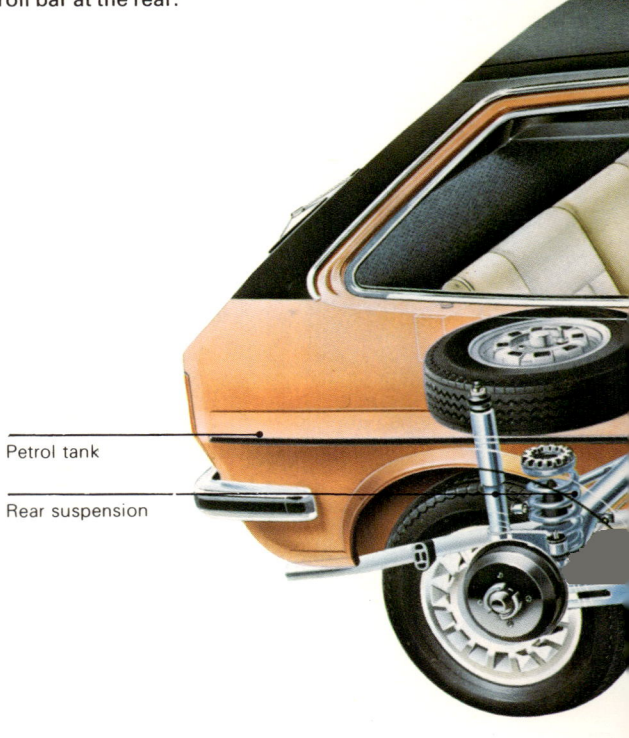

---

diaphragm while at the same time allowing suction from the inlet manifold to create a partial vacuum on the other side. The diaphragm therefore moves and a rod attached to the diaphragm presses against the piston in the master cylinder, thus amplifying the effort used in depressing the brake pedal. Some brake servo systems use the vacuum to assist the depression of the pedal directly, rather than the master cylinder piston.
Shaft drive is the system of transmitting the power of the engine using gears, UNIVERSAL JOINTS and rotating solid metal shafts.
Shoulder of the road is a continuation of the base course (see PAVEMENT) on either side of the riding surface.
Silencer is a chamber in the exhaust pipe in which the waste gases are allowed to expand and the noise released during expansion is reduced. In a baffle silencer the plates, or baffles, increase the distance travelled by the gases. A straight-through silencer, which causes less reduction in engine power, contains a perforated tube surrounded by a sound-absorbent material.
Solenoid switch is an electro-magnetic device used in starting. When the ignition switch is turned, current from the battery flows through the coil of the solenoid. This causes a metal plunger to make contact with the two terminals connected to the BATTERY and STARTER MOTOR. Thus the large current needed to turn the motor does not have to flow down the long cables to the ignition switch.
Spark plug contains a central core of metal, or inner electrode, connected to a terminal at the top. This electrode is insulated by a ceramic material from the metal plug casing, or outer electrode. At the base the 2 electrodes are separated only by a small gap — the spark gap. The terminal is connected to 1 of the leads from the DISTRIBUTOR and the metal casing screws into the cylinder head, which is connected through the car body to the earth terminal of the BATTERY. A pulse of high voltage current from the distributor discharges, causing a spark to pass across the spark gap.

Speedometer

Travelling by Road

includes a set of DIFFERENTIAL gears. This allows the wheels at the ends of the two drive shafts to revolve at different speeds when the car is turning a corner.

In some front-wheel drive cars the engine and gearbox are mounted transversely (across the car) and power is transmitted from the gearbox directly to a differential gear system. From this a drive shaft, connected at both ends by universal joints, leads to each wheel.

The suspension system is needed to provide a comfortable ride and to keep the wheels on the road. The earliest form of suspension, used on carriages in the 1800s, was the leaf spring. This is still used in cars, particularly on the rear axles. Other forms of suspension include rubber, air, fluid-gas and coiled metal springs and torsion (twisting) bars, generally in conjunction with hydraulic shock absorbers to damp down the movement of the springs.

Several different types of steering mechanism are used but they all work on a principle first devised in the 1700s. Before the 1700s the axle pivoted in the centre, but in the new system the turning action of the steering wheel caused the axle to slide to the right or left and so change the direction of the wheels which were pivoted at each end of the axle. Power steering, used on many modern cars, uses oil under pressure to assist the movement of the steering mechanism.

For braking, cars use drum brakes, disc brakes or both. A common system uses drum brakes on

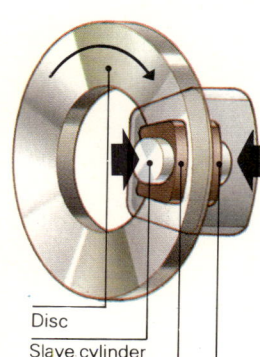

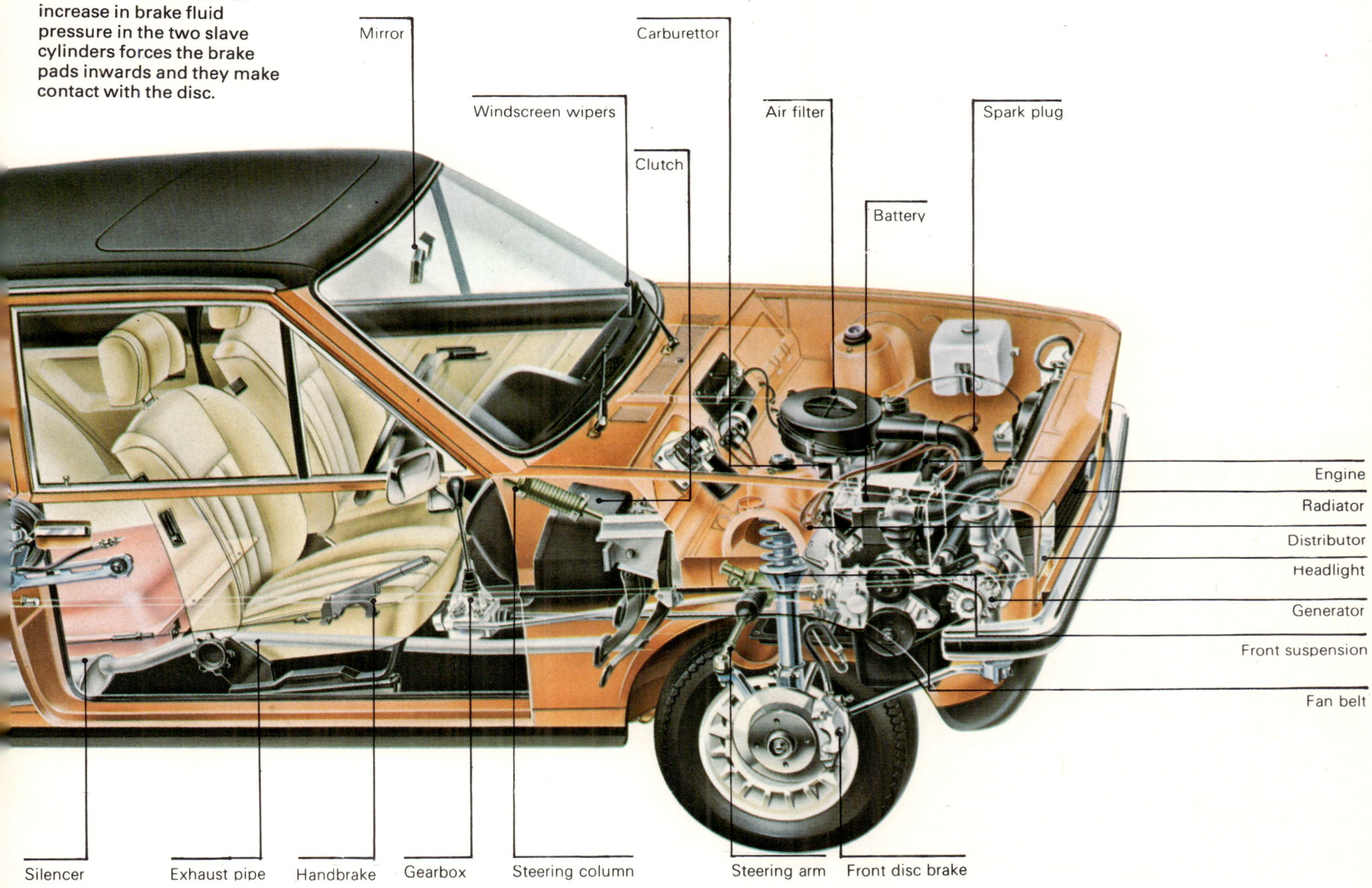

Above: In a disc brake an increase in brake fluid pressure in the two slave cylinders forces the brake pads inwards and they make contact with the disc.

Speedometer is driven from a point on the transmission that rotates at a speed directly proportional to the speed of the wheels. A flexible drive cable rotates a magnet inside a metal drum. The drum, which is connected to the speedometer indicator needle, also tries to turn in the magnetic field, but is prevented from turning very far by a coiled spring. However, the faster the magnet rotates the further the drum and needle move round. A speedometer generally also incorporates an odometer, which measures the distance travelled.
Sprocket is a small, toothed wheel, which can be turned by a roller chain; the rollers fit in between the teeth.
Starter motor is the electric motor used to turn the CRANKSHAFT during the process of starting the engine. When the motor turns, a pinion moves along a screw-threaded shaft and engages the teeth on the FLYWHEEL. When the engine fires, the pinion is driven back along the shaft and disengages.
Steering system consists of a steering wheel and column linked to the wheels. In a rack and pinion steering system a pinion (see GEARS) on the end of the column moves the rack, which is a flat, toothed rod linked to the steering rods, from side to side. In a worm and peg system a worm gear, turned by the column, moves a peg backwards or forwards. The peg is linked by arms to the steering rods.
Subgrade of a road is the soil or rock on which the PAVEMENT is laid.
Supercharger is a device for increasing the amount and pressure of air and fuel taken into the cylinders so that more fuel is burned. Some types are driven by the engine via belts and pulleys; turbochargers use a turbine which is driven by the exhaust gases.
Suspension wheel works on the principle that a heavy weight will hang safely from a thin, light wire. Thus, in a bicycle the weight of the rider and bicycle is made to hang from the top of the wheels rather than stand on thick spokes.
Throttle, see CARBURETTOR.
Transmission is the means by which engine power is transferred to the wheels.

Steering wheel and column

Travelling by Road

Left: The Dover end of the Channel Tunnel, which was intended to link England and France. The project was abandoned in 1975, owing to rising costs. However, if it is ever built, the chalk rock beneath the English Channel will be easy to dig through and will require very little support.

Below right: A bridge has to withstand its own weight and that of any traffic it might carry. The longer the bridge's span, the greater the load it must bear.
1. A beam bridge needs several supports to carry the load.
2. In an arch bridge the load is directed outwards along the arch.
3. The load of a suspension bridge is held by the two main supports and cables attached to the banks.
4. In a cantilever bridge the main load is carried by the supports. The load in the middle of the long span is held by the arms attached to the bank.

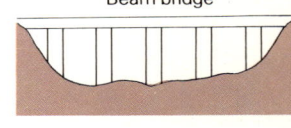
Beam bridge

Arch bridge

Suspension bridge

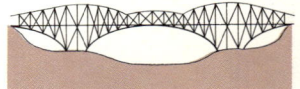
Cantilever bridge

the rear wheels and disc brakes on the front. The brakes are operated hydraulically. Pressing down on the foot pedal increases pressure in a fluid-filled master cylinder. This is transmitted through pipes to the smaller slave cylinder in each brake. In a drum brake two brake shoes are pushed outwards to make contact with the inside of a brake drum. In a disc brake the disc is gripped by two brake pads. In some cars the brakes are SERVO-ASSISTED by a system that uses the vacuum created in the engine's inlet MANIFOLD. Most cars have a secondary system called a HANDBRAKE.

The fuel system consists of a petrol tank, fuel pump and CARBURETTOR. The function of the carburettor is to vaporize the petrol, mix the petrol vapour with the correct proportion of air and to supply the engine with the required amount of this mixture.

The exhaust system carries away the waste gases from the engine and consists of a long pipe connected to the exhaust manifold. Some way along the pipe a SILENCER is fitted and this reduces the noise of the expanding gases.

The electrical system consists of a number of components. The BATTERY supplies power for the lights, wipers and other equipment and also for starting. When the starter switch is operated the electric STARTER MOTOR turns the engine, drawing in fuel from the carburettor. At the same time the coil produces a high tension (high voltage) current which flows to the DISTRIBUTOR. The rotor arm of the distributor is turned by a mechanical connection to the camshaft of the engine and feeds the current to each spark plug via four leads. When the engine is idling, the battery provides all the power. At higher speeds an engine-driven GENERATOR provides the necessary current and recharges the battery.

Roads, bridges and tunnels

The first roads developed from the tracks and paths trodden by Stone Age man. The increase in trade between settlements that resulted from the arrival of the wheel meant that such tracks had to be improved. Roadways were levelled and ditches were dug at the sides to provide drainage.

Stone roads appeared in China in about 3500 BC and in the Mediterranean area in about 1500 BC while at the same time in northern Europe log roads were in use. Many of these roads formed long trade routes. But the Romans were the first to build a system of scientifically constructed roads. They built more than 85,000 kilometres of road, linking the various parts of their Empire. These long, straight roads were constructed in several layers, topped with paving stones set in mortar.

After the decline of the Roman Empire, the roadways of Europe fell into disrepair and only began to improve again in the late 1600s. The STAGECOACHES (*see page 5*) ran on stone-surfaced toll roads built on much the same principle as the massive Roman roads. The French roads of the late 1700s were the best in Europe. In 1775 Pierre Tresuaget devised the modern method of road construction in which the load is carried by the soil underneath the road instead of by the surface of the road itself.

Three British engineers also made major contributions to road building. John Metcalf, who built many roads in the mid-1700s, stressed the importance of good drainage. Thomas

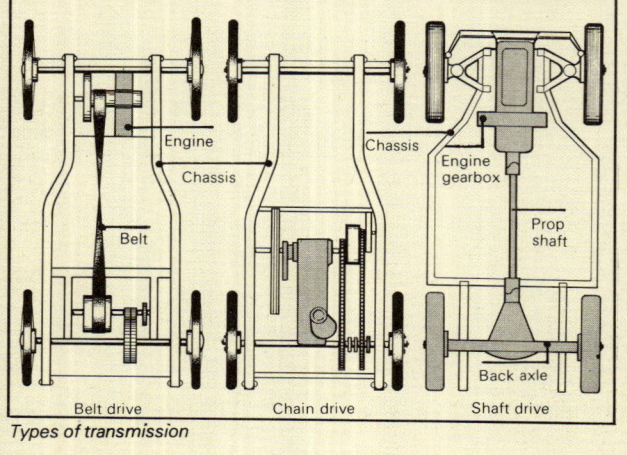
Types of transmission

See AUTOMATIC TRANSMISSION and SHAFT DRIVE.
Trunk roads, or arterial roads, carry long distance traffic, avoiding city centres.
Two-stroke cycle is a system of engine operation in which every second stroke of the piston is the power stroke. Each stroke combines 2 of the strokes of a 4-stroke cycle. On the upstroke fuel and air mixture is drawn into the crankcase through the inlet port. Towards the end of the upstroke the mixture in the cylinder is compressed. Combustion of the fuel begins the downstroke, or power stroke, and towards the end of the downstroke fuel mixture passes into the cylinder through a transfer passage, forcing the waste gases out through the exhaust port.
Tyres are inflatable rubber rings round the wheels of a car. They have flexible sidewalls and thick treads, which are grooved for draining away water. Some tyres have an inner tube, but today most tyres are tubeless, having a soft rubber lining which forms a seal between the wheel rim and the tyre. Inside the outer rubber layer of a tyre there is a casing made of layers (plies) of fabric. A cross-ply tyre is so-called because the cords (threads) used to run across the tyre (at right angles to the direction of rotation). Today, however, cross-ply cords run at an angle of 40° or less. In a radial-ply tyre the cords run across the tyre, and there is a layer of breaker plies, with diagonally-running cords, underneath the tread.

U **Universal joint**, or Hooke joint, consists of 2 yokes (forks on the ends of

Travelling by Road

Roman road

Modern light-vehicle road

Modern heavy-vehicle road

Telford in the late 1700s emphasized the need for solid foundations. In 1816 John McAdam devised a method of surface construction that used small stones compacted together. Roads that use this type of hard surface are still referred to as macadamized roads.

Above: A Roman road had a foundation of stone blocks set in mortar. Above this was a layer of smaller stones bound together with cement. The surface was made up of close-fitting stone blocks. A modern road used by light traffic has a sub-base course of large stones. Above this is a base course of ash or gravel, well rolled down. The surface is tarmacadam (small stones bound together with tar or asphalt). A modern road used by heavy traffic, such as a motorway, may have a base course of reinforced concrete. Above this is a layer of waterproof paper. The surface is another layer of concrete, perhaps topped with asphalt.

Modern roads, built for cars and heavy lorries, have hard, cambered (rounded) surfaces and solid, load-bearing foundations composed of several layers. Each layer spreads the load over a wider area, so that the underlying soil, or subgrade, does not subside under the weight of the traffic above. The surface of the road may be asphalt, a mixture of bitumen and fine stone chips, or concrete reinforced with steel mesh.

Bridges for spanning rivers and similar obstacles have been in use for thousands of years. The simplest beam bridge consists of a plank across a small stream, and suspension bridges in the form of log footways suspended over ravines are still in use in some parts of the world. Stone and wooden arch bridges were first used by the Romans. During the Industrial Revolution bridges that could carry enormous weights became necessary. The large iron bridges that were built were tremendous feats of engineering.

Modern bridges are built from steel and reinforced concrete, materials which allow them to have both wide spans and elegant constructions. Large beam bridges use several beams supported by a number of piers. A cantilever bridge is a type of beam bridge in which the number of piers is reduced. The beams project out from the tops of the piers and are fixed at each end, either to the bank or to the ends of other cantilevered beams. In a suspension bridge the roadway is suspended by steel ropes from cables which pass over towers and are then anchored to the ground.

Tunnels are bored where hills and mountains are too steep to pass over. The Romans were the first to build tunnels, using picks and shovels. Tunnelling became easier with the discovery of explosives, but today it is mostly done with machinery. Tunnels are more common on railways than on roads, as trains have more difficulty than cars in negotiating steep inclines.

Left: From above, the Harbor Freeway in Los Angeles, USA, can be seen as a dual carriageway with single carriageway roads crossing over it. The minor roads are connected to the freeway by curving link roads.

shafts) pivoted on a central, cross-shaped spider. Both shafts can rotate even if there is a small angle between them. However, if the angle becomes too great, the velocity of one shaft becomes greater than the velocity of the other. On modern front-wheel drive cars this problem is solved by using special kinds of universal joints called constant velocity joints.

V Valves are mushroom-shaped pieces of metal used to open and close the inlet and exhaust ports of a 4-stroke engine. They are operated by the CAMSHAFT. In an engine with overhead valves and a camshaft in the cylinder block the movement of a cam is transferred to a tappet, which rests on the cam. In the tappet there is a push rod, which is linked to one end of a rocker arm above the cylinder head. The other end of the rocker arm, which pivots on the rocker shaft, touches the top of a valve stem. Thus when the tappet and push rod are moved upwards by the cam the valve is lowered and the port is opened. The port is closed by a spring fixed to the valve stem. In side-valve and overhead camshaft engines the tappet operates the valve stem directly.

Verrazano Narrows Bridge, completed in 1964, is the longest suspension bridge in the world. Its main span is 1,298 metres long and it bridges the entrance to New York harbour. It has 2 decks and carries 12 lanes of road traffic. Its 4 main cables are each 90 cm in diameter.

Y Yerbo Bueno Island Tunnel, San Francisco, has the largest diameter of any tunnel in the world. It is 17 metres high, 23 metres wide and 165 metres long. It carries 2 decks of traffic.

Verrazano Narrows Bridge

Most canal construction ended when the golden age of the railways began. But some canals, such as the Panama Canal, the St Lawrence Seaway and the Suez Canal, are still vital arteries of world trade.

Canals

Canals are man-made waterways used for water transport and irrigation or drainage. No-one knows how canals first evolved, but in hot countries large irrigation ditches could have carried small boats and eventually people probably realized the advantages of transporting heavy loads by water. The earliest known canals were built in Mesopotamia in about 5000 BC.

The early canals could only pass over flat areas of land. If the countryside became hilly the canals could not be made to rise with it. However, when locks were introduced, it became possible for canals to cross several different levels of countryside. The Chinese used a simple kind of lock in about AD 100. This consisted of a weir — a dam over which water falls — in which there was a removable gate, called a flash lock. A boat moving from the higher level to the lower would hurtle down with the rush of water when the gate was opened. A boat moving in the other direction had to be winched up against the flow.

In the late 900s the Chinese were using two flash locks together, thus inventing the modern pound, or chamber, lock. This consists of two gates in between which is a chamber of water. The level of the water in the chamber can be altered to either of the two levels at each end of the lock. The early Chinese chamber lock used guillotine gates. These could be raised to allow water to flow in or out of the lock. Similar locks were in use in Europe by the late 1300s.

Most modern locks have mitre gates, a system invented by Leonardo da Vinci in 1487 for a canal in Milan, Italy. At each end of the lock

Right: The entrance to the canal tunnel at Worsley, the start of the original Bridgewater canal. Inspired by a visit to the Canal du Midi in France, Francis Egerton, Duke of Bridgewater, commissioned James Brindley to build a canal to carry coal to Manchester from his estate at Worsley. In this scene an early form of crane is being used to load a barge. The canal was later extended to the River Mersey at Runcorn.

Reference

B **Briare Canal**, built by Hugues Cosnier in 1642, was the first true summit-level canal. From Briare it rises 39 metres to a summit plateau 6.2 km long. From there it drops 81 metres to join the River Loing at Rogny. It has 40 locks and at one point between the summit and Rogny 6 of these form a staircase that drops 20 metres.

Bridgewater Canal was the first of many canals built in Britain in the 1700s. These included the Grand Trunk Canal, which linked the Mersey to the Trent, the Grand Union Canal, which linked the Grand Trunk Canal with the Thames, and the Severn Waterway and Gloucester and Sharpness Canal, which provided the final link from the Thames to the Bristol Channel.

C **Caledonian Ship Canal** was built by the Scottish engineer Thomas Telford (1757–1834) between 1803 and 1822. It linked Loch Lochy and Loch Ness along the line of the Great Glen of Scotland with Loch Linnhe (sea) in the west and the Moray Firth in the east. Built so that sailing ships could avoid the long and hazardous journey round Cape Wrath, it soon became obsolete when steam power arrived and ships increased in size.

Canal du Midi, also known as the Languedoc Canal, was built by Paul Riquet between 1666 and 1685. It links the River Garonne, which flows into the sea at Bordeaux, with the Mediterranean Sea via the Bassin de Thau at

Corinth Canal

Sète. From Toulouse it uses 26 locks to rise 61 metres in 54 km to the summit. The descent to the sea is a drop of 185 metres over 190 km, and 74 locks are used for this. Riquet went to great lengths to ensure that the summit had sufficient water and built a dam and over 60 km of feeder channels.

Corinth Canal in Greece is a deep sea-to-sea ship canal that connects the Ionian Sea via the Gulf of Corinth to the Aegean Sea, saving the long journey round the Peloponnisos. The canal was first attempted in about AD 60 by

there is a pair of wooden gates hinged to the sides of the chamber. When they close they form a V-shape. The name 'mitre', a carpenter's term, refers to the join between the two gates when they are closed. The V-shape points upstream so that the water pressure helps to seal the gates more effectively. The greatest pressure on the gates, and hence the most effective seal, occurs when there is a difference in water level on either side of the gates.

Many of the early canals follow a wandering course. The reason for this is that the engineering techniques needed to cross high ground were not available. However, since the 1600s several methods have been used to overcome such problems. Tunnels were bored through hills and tall viaducts crossed over valleys. In high-rise canals, water was pumped to the top in order to maintain the water level of the higher locks. Step locks consist of a series of locks. The lower gate of each lock acts as the upper gate of the next. Boat lifts are used to haul boats up slopes, either in tanks of water or on trolleys, from one level to another. A modern lift at Montech in France pushes boats up in a pool of water sealed by a movable dam. In some places boats are lifted down from one canal to another canal or river.

Above: A horse-drawn barge on the Grand Western Canal, Devon, where it crosses (by means of an aqueduct) the disused Tiverton branch railway line.

Below: A chamber, or pound, lock. First the upper gates and sluices close. The lower sluices open and water falls to the lower level. Then the lower gates open and a boat enters the chamber. The lower gates close and upper sluices open to let water rise to the upper level. The upper gates open and the boat leaves.

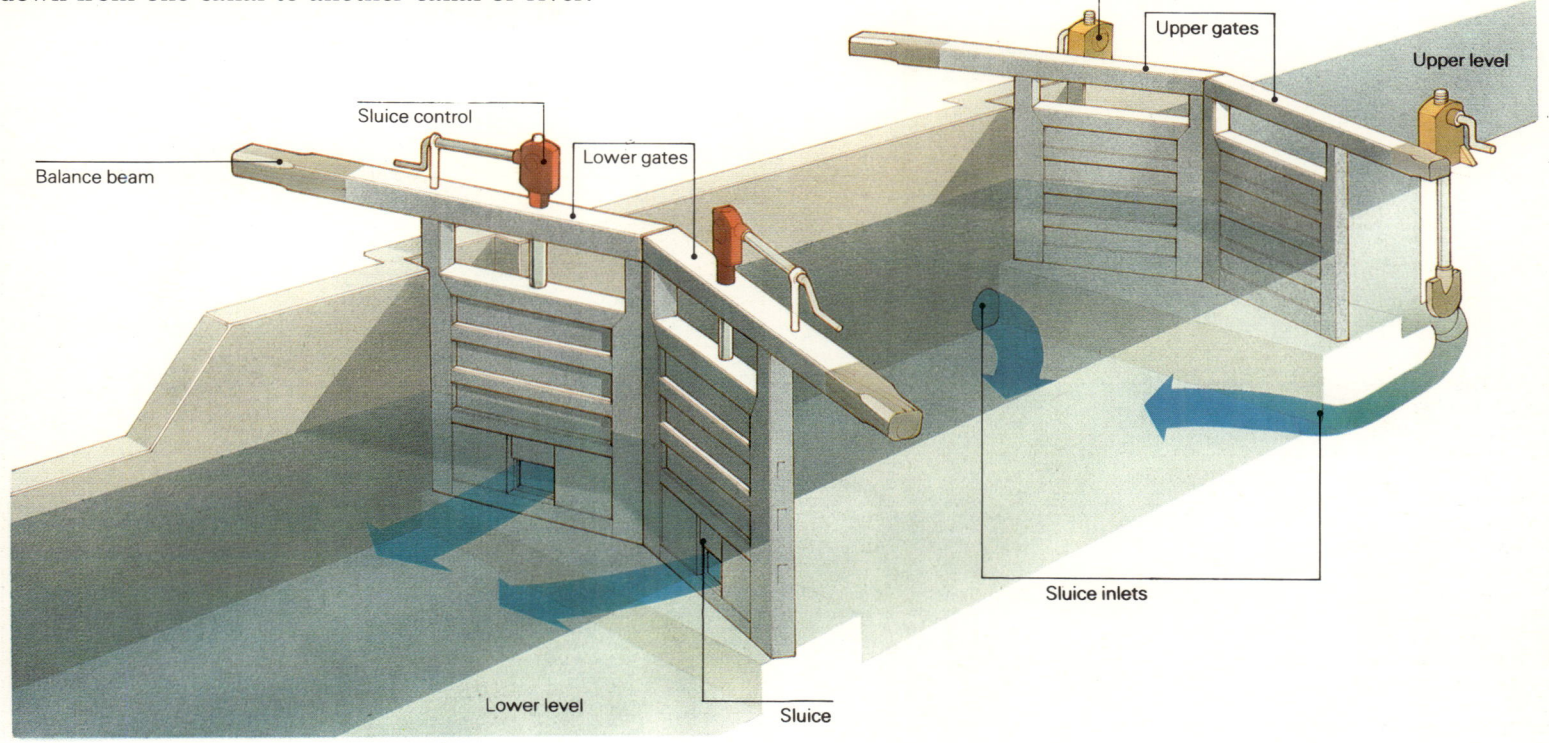

the Roman Emperor Nero. In the late 1800s the shafts he had begun were reopened and continued. The 6.3-km canal is today an awesome sight. Its almost vertical, sheer cliffs, cut through solid rock, rise 86 metres above the water. Being only 8 metres deep and 25 metres wide the canal can only take vessels of up to 10,000 tonnes and the largest ships have to be towed through with care.

D **Dry dock** is used when the hull of a ship needs to be inspected or repaired. As the dock is pumped dry, the ship comes to rest on keel blocks arranged to fit the shape of the hull. Modern dry docks often have guidance systems so that the ship is accurately positioned on the blocks. Most dry docks take one ship at a time, but the largest dry dock in the world, the Lisnave dock, Lisbon, Portugal, can take two or more ships. It is 518 metres long, 97 metres wide and 16.15 metres deep.

E **Erie Canal** is 580 km long and has 82 locks. Built between 1817 and 1825, it links Buffalo on Lake Erie with Albany on the River Hudson. This canal eased the flow of produce from the mid-west prairies to New York and, when it was opened, was the longest canal in the world (580 km).

F **Floating dock** is a form of dry dock. The dock is first submerged and the ship positioned above it. Water is then pumped out of ballast tanks and the dock rises, lifting the ship with it. Some floating docks can lift ships of up to 80,000 tonnes.

P **Panama Canal** was first thought of by Ferdinand de Lesseps after his success with the SUEZ CANAL. He proposed a sea-level canal via Lake Nicaragua, but in attempting this project between 1881 and 1889 he was beaten by the terrain and the climate. He then began a

The de Lesseps attempt to dig the Panama Canal

Inland canals became popular in Europe between the 1600s and 1800s. Two French canals were among the greatest engineering achievements of their time. The BRIARE CANAL, completed in 1642, linked the River Loire and the River Seine. The CANAL DU MIDI, completed in 1681, linked the River Garonne with the Mediterranean. This canal inspired the building of the BRIDGEWATER CANAL between Worsley and Manchester in England in 1761, which began a 70-year era of canal construction in Britain during the Industrial Revolution. This was brought to an end by the coming of the railways. Only the Manchester Ship Canal (1894) was built after this period.

The success of the European canals showed the Americans the possibilities of inland water transport. In 1825 the ERIE CANAL, between Buffalo and Albany, was built, and in 1829 the WELLAND CANAL by-passed the Niagara Falls between Lake Ontario and Lake Erie. A series of later canals linked the Great Lakes with the Mississippi, Ohio and Susquehanna Rivers and, finally, in 1959 the whole inland waterway system was linked to the sea via the ST LAWRENCE SEAWAY.

In addition to inland waterways, several sea-to-sea ship canals have been built. The most famous of these is the SUEZ CANAL, built by the French engineer Ferdinand de Lesseps (1805–94) and opened in 1869. Other major ship canals include the CORINTH CANAL (1893) and the PANAMA CANAL (1914). However, most of the early ship canals are now too narrow to take modern ships. The CALEDONIAN SHIP CANAL (1822), for example, is obsolete. Only the Suez Canal, which has no locks and crosses desert, has been relatively easy to enlarge.

The tremendous increase in the size of ships has created similar problems in docks. The early docks, built to take the steamships of the 1800s, are not large enough for modern container ships. Thus new docks have had to be built.

A dock is an area in which ships can be moored and loaded or unloaded, generally alongside a quay. The quay is often equipped with cranes and rails for railway wagons. Many modern docks have facilities for handling containerized goods and wheeled freight or passenger transport that can roll off or on a ship via an opening in the bow or stern.

Right: A tanker on the Welland Canal passing under a vertical lift bridge. The tanker is on its way from the Great Lakes to the sea via the St Lawrence Seaway.

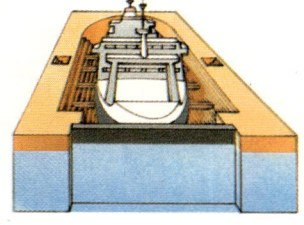

Above: A dry dock. The ship is floated into the dock and positioned over the hull supports. The steel gate is then floated into place and sunk and the water is pumped out of the dock.

In many places the tides do not affect the working of the dock. For example, in Melbourne, Australia, the water rises only 1 metre during a spring tide (the most extreme form of tide). However, in places where the difference between high and low tides is much greater, docks have to be enclosed by an entrance lock. An extreme example of tidal variation occurs at Bristol in England, where the difference between high and low water can be as much as 15 metres. However, inside the enclosed docks ships remain in deep water and can leave or enter at any time via the locks. A DRY DOCK is simply a basin that can be pumped dry.

Early docks all had mitre gates similar to those used on canals. Modern lock gates, which have to be deeper than those of the 1800s, are of various kinds. Some are mitre gates; others are flap gates, hinged at the lower end; others are traversing caissons, which move sideways on rails; and others are caissons, which are floated into place and then filled with water to sink them.

---

canal across the narrowest point of the isthmus at Panama, but was again forced to abandon it owing to problems with the rock strata and the malaria and yellow fever contracted by his workmen. The American government remained interested in such a canal, but political problems, concerned with who had the right to build, maintain and regulate it, delayed the project for several years. Work began in 1904 and the canal was finally completed in 1914. It is 85 km long, 91.5 metres wide and 8.2 metres deep. Between Libon Bay in the Caribbean Sea and Balboa on the Pacific coast it rises 22 metres to the Gatun Lake, which is the main source of the canal's water supply.

S St Lawrence Seaway was built to open up 3,830 km of navigable waterway between the head of Lake Superior and the Atlantic Ocean. Work on the seaway began in 1954 and it was opened in 1959. From Montreal harbour at the head of the St Lawrence River it rises 52 metres to Lake Ontario, bypassing the Lachine rapids and the International rapids. From Lake Ontario, the WELLAND CANAL leads to Lake Erie, 45 km away. From there, 2 canals with locks form the final links with Lake Huron and Lake Superior.

Suez Canal is a sea-to-sea ship canal that provides a link between the Mediterranean and the Red Sea. The canal was first dug during the early Egyptian civilization, but fell into disuse and had become blocked by about AD 700. In 1854 the Frenchman Ferdinand de Lesseps was granted a concession to build a new canal. Work began in 1859 and was completed in 10 years. It is a sea-level canal 169 km long

Suez Canal, 1869

and has no locks. Originally 60 metres wide and 7.5 metres deep, it was enlarged in 1954 to 150 metres wide with a main channel 13 metres deep in order to accommodate the growing number of larger ships.

W Welland Canal, which links Lake Erie and Lake Ontario, was originally built with 40 locks. In 1912 it was improved as an early part of the St Lawrence Seaway project and the 98-metre rise was covered by 8 locks, each 236 metres long, 24 metres wide and 8 metres deep.

In 1829 George Stephenson's locomotive, the *Rocket*, reached the then unheard of speed of 58 km/ hour. Today Japanese 'lightning trains' reach 210 km/ hour, providing the world's fastest regular service.

The Railway Revolution

The various components of railways, such as tracks, locomotives and wagons, were all invented at different times for different purposes. They were brought together at the beginning of the 1800s, when England was in the middle of the Industrial Revolution, to satisfy the urgent need for an efficient method of transporting large quantities of goods.

The result revolutionized everyone's way of life. Because goods could be moved cheaply and easily, industry flourished and new towns grew up. The railways offered speed and ease of transport and many more people could now afford the time and money to travel. Gradually, people realized that they could live in the country and work in the town. Thus our modern way of life – a way of life that thousands of commuters, businessmen and holidaymakers now take for granted – has been shaped for us by the railways.

Tracks, horses and steam

The idea of using tracks originated in mines during the 1500s. Hauling a wagon along the uneven floor of a mine was nearly impossible and so two parallel rows of planks were laid down for the wheels to run on. To keep the wagon on the planks a vertical bar ran in the central gap. Wooden rails were soon invented and some mines had wagons with flanged wheels, like those of modern railcars, to keep them on the rails.

When iron wheels came into use, in the early 1700s, it was found that they wore down the wooden rails, and iron rails were introduced. At the same time, mine railways were being extended to carry coal to nearby wharves on rivers and, later, canals. Where the railway was on a suitable slope the loaded wagons were allowed to roll down to the wharf. In other places horses were used to pull trains of wagons.

All these early railways were private works or mine lines. In 1803 the first public line, the Surrey Iron Railway, was opened. It carried goods between Wandsworth and Croydon. The first horse-drawn passenger line, the Oystermouth Railway, was opened four years later and carried passengers between Oystermouth and Swansea. Horse-drawn trains continued to operate for a number of years, particularly in France, where steam power did not arrive until the 1830s, and in America, where they survived on short lines long after the arrival of steam-powered locomotives.

Steam power was first discovered by the Greek engineer HERO in about AD 50. His 'steam engine' worked on the same principle as a modern lawn sprinkler. Jets of steam from two bent tubes attached to a hollow sphere filled with boiling water caused the sphere to revolve. However, slave labour was cheap and the idea of using steam power for doing useful work did not occur to anyone until the late 1600s. The French

Below: As long ago as the 1500s wooden trucks in mines had flanged wheels that ran on wooden rails. Flanged wheels are still used today to keep rolling stock on the rails.

Reference

A Abt, Roman (1850–1933) was a Swiss locomotive engineer. Having trained under RIGGENBACH he became chief engineer of the International Company for Mountain Railways in 1875. In 1882 he devised his rack rail system. This was a great improvement on previous systems as the rack consisted of a single upright plate into which the rack slots were machined. By 1929 there were 72 railways using this system.

Arthur Kill Bridge is a vertical lift bridge that links Staten Island, New York, with New Jersey. The 170-metre lifting span remains horizontal as it is raised by counterweights at each end.

Articulated steam locomotives have 2 sets of cylinders each driving an independent set of wheels. The frames on which the wheel axles revolve are hinged together and the assembly supports the boiler.

B Best Friend of Charleston began the first steam passenger service in America on Christmas Day 1830 on the South Carolina Railroad. This was an American-built locomotive with a vertical boiler and it hauled regular traffic from January to June 1831, when the boiler exploded. Parts of the locomotive were used in another locomotive, the *Phoenix*.

Blucher, built in 1814, was George STEPHENSON's first locomotive. Its vertical cylin-

Locomotive, The Best Friend of Charleston, *December, 1830*

physicist Denis PAPIN discovered that expanding steam could be used to force a piston up a tube. In 1698 he built a model steam engine in which the piston was forced up by steam and pushed back by the air pressure on the other side when the cylinder was cooled.

One of the problems in early mines was flooding and pumping water out by hand was hard work and very slow. In the same year as Papin built his model engine, Thomas SAVERY, an English engineer, built a machine that drew water up by creating a vacuum in a chamber at the top of a pipe. The vacuum was caused by filling the chamber with steam and then cooling it, thus condensing the steam to a few drops of water. The vacuum sucked the water some way up the pipe and then steam pressure was used to blow the water out completely. There were no moving parts and the movements of water and steam were controlled by valves. Savery's steam pump was used in mines, but it employed steam under high pressure and was liable to explode.

In 1712 another English engineer, Thomas NEWCOMEN, invented a better steam pump. It worked on the same principle as Savery's, but the steam pressure and vacuum were used to make a piston move up and down, as in Papin's engine. The piston was attached to one end of a rocking beam, the other end of which was fitted to a water pump. Newcomen's pump was thus the first engine to convert heat energy into useful mechanical energy. The steam was under fairly low pressure and so the machine was not as dangerous as Savery's. Newcomen's steam pumps were used in mines for many years. The last was dismantled in 1934.

However, the most important advance in the development of steam engines was made by the Scottish engineer James WATT. In 1764, after repairing a Newcomen engine, he realized how inefficient it was. The steam in the cylinder had to be cooled down on each stroke and enormous amounts of steam were needed to heat it up again. Watt built an improved steam engine with a separate condenser. Thus the cylinder always remained hot. By 1769 Watt had developed a much more efficient engine than Newcomen's. As a further improvement, instead of using a vacuum he devised a system of moving the piston by introducing steam first to one side and then the other. In 1774 he began manufacturing his machines and by 1800 he had sold about 500. In 1781 he added a system of mechanical cranks and levers that converted the back-and-forth

Right: A pithead scene in about 1820 showing the Newcomen engine used to pump water out of the mine. A coal fire was used to boil the water in the large round boiler. Steam was fed to the cylinder, causing the piston to rise and thus pushing one end of the wooden beam upwards. When the piston reached the top of the cylinder, the steam condensed, leaving a partial vacuum. Atmospheric pressure pushed the piston down again and the other end of the beam rose. This end was attached to the water pump.

ders were linked by connecting rods and cranks to gears, which turned the wheels. At one time it had a chain drive to the front wheels of the tender.

Blue Train, inaugurated in 1939, runs between Cape Town and Pretoria in South Africa and is the most luxurious train in the world. Passengers travel in private rooms for the whole of the 26-hour journey and the carriages run silently with no vibration. The service is like that of a first class hotel.

Brakes, in the early days of railways, were hand-operated levers on each wagon. In the late 1800s, two automatic brake systems came into use, the American Westinghouse air brake and the British vacuum brake. They are operated by the driver in the locomotive and tread or disc brakes act on all the wheels of the coaches. If a coach is disconnected from the locomotive its brakes are automatically applied.

Britannia Bridge, the first iron box-girder bridge, was built across the Menai Straits in North Wales between 1845 and 1850 by Robert STEPHENSON. It was originally designed as a suspension bridge, but Stephenson used plate girders to build two long tubes and during construction he found that the supporting cables were unnecessary. Trains ran inside the tubes across four spans. The two longest spans over the water measured 140 metres. In 1970 the bridge was destroyed by fire and replaced with a steel arch bridge.

Section of Britannia Bridge

Brunel, Isambard Kingdom (1806–59) was the son of Sir Marc Isambard BRUNEL. He trained under his father and assisted in building the Rotherhithe Tunnel in London. Between 1829 and 1831 he designed the Clifton Suspension Bridge over the Avon Gorge in Bristol. Lack of funds delayed the work and others completed the construction. Between 1833 and 1841 he laid out the 188-km Great Western Railway line from London to Bristol, building a magnificent series of bridges and tunnels. He also designed a few locomotives, which were not successful. But despite his railway achievements Brunel was not primarily a railway engineer. His motive for building the Great Western Railway was to provide a railway link as part of the journey from London to New York. To provide the sea link

The Railway Revolution

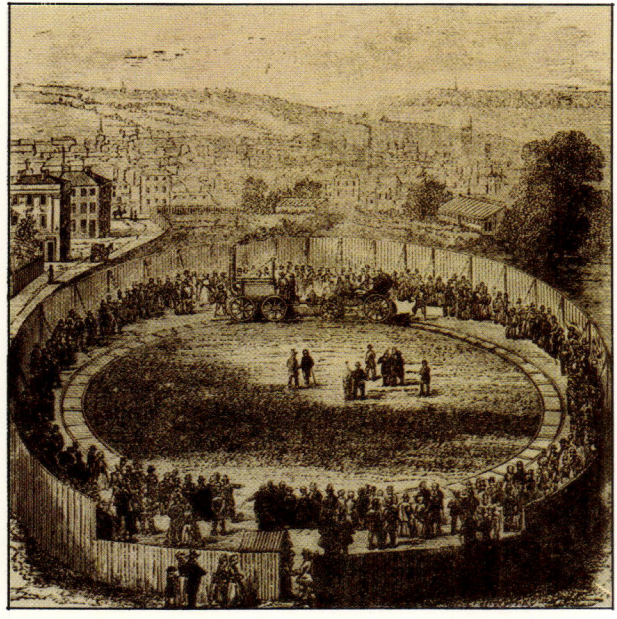

Above: Before the arrival of steam power, trains were drawn by horses. This print shows the railway from St Etienne to Lyons in 1829. Later, the line was the first in France to use steam locomotives, although at first only for goods trains.

Left: Trevithick's circular track in north London in 1808. He charged passengers a shilling a ride in a coach pulled by *Catch-me-who-can*, his fourth locomotive. This was 22 years before the first permanent steam passenger railway was built.

movement of the piston into the rotary movement of a wheel. Watt's steam engines, developed just when they were needed in the middle of the Industrial Revolution, came to be used in factories all over England.

With Watt's invention steam transport became possible. Steam road carriages, such as those built by the English inventor Richard TREVITHICK and others, appeared on the roads (*see page 17*). But they had only limited success and it was at this point that steam engines and railway tracks were brought together. At first, stationary steam engines were used to haul wagons up slopes by cable. Then in 1803 Trevithick developed the first steam locomotive. Engineering technology had improved since the days of Savery, and Trevithick found that he could use steam under high pressure and do away with the condenser used by Watt, thus making the whole engine lighter. In 1804 Trevithick's second locomotive, PENYDARRAN, successfully hauled a loaded train both ways along 14.4 kilometres of railway in South Wales.

Trevithick demonstrated his fourth locomotive, *Catch-me-who-can*, on a circular track in London in 1808. He advertized it as 'Trevithick's travelling machine without horses, impelled by steam' and it was the first occasion on which a train pulled by a steam locomotive carried fare-paying passengers, albeit round in circles! Unfortunately, Trevithick, already plagued by bad luck in his numerous experiments, could not interest anyone with sufficient money to back him and he gave up.

By this time, however, others had caught on to the idea of steam traction on railways. In 1812, John Blenkinsop (1783–1831) had four locomotives that successfully ran on a rack railway at the Middleton colliery near Leeds. These locomotives were the forerunners of those that run on the rack railways in mountain areas today. In 1814, William Hedley (1779–1843) built the PUFFING BILLY at the Wylam colliery on the River Tyne. This locomotive, and the two others that were built soon after it, did not use the rack system, relying on the natural grip between the rails and the wheels.

The success of these locomotives prompted other mine owners to build steam railways and the English inventor George STEPHENSON was commissioned to build a railway at Killingworth colliery. His first locomotive, the BLUCHER, was a success and he went on to build several more locomotives for use in collieries.

Stephenson was not only an excellent engineer. He also had the vision to see the prospect of a Britain criss-crossed with railway lines. His enthusiasm and shrewd tactics aroused the interest of others, and in 1821 he was appointed chief engineer of the Stockton and Darlington Railway. This, the first public steam railway, was built to carry coal from Durham to the coast. There was no canal and so there was no competition. It was opened on September 27 1825 with a train of passenger-carrying wagons pulled by Stephenson's latest locomotive, LOCOMOTION, built for the occasion.

Stephenson's most famous locomotive is the ROCKET. The design of this locomotive added

---

he built 3 great steamships. The *Great Western*, built between 1837 and 1838, operated the first scheduled transatlantic service. The *Great Britain*, built between 1843 and 1845, was the first iron steamship and the first fitted with a screw propeller. The 12,000-tonne *Great Eastern* was not a commercial success, but in 1866 was used to lay the first transatlantic cable.

Brunel, Sir Marc Isambard (1769–1849) was a civil engineer. Born in France, he settled in England in 1799. He devised an early form of mass-production for making naval pulley blocks. In 1818 he devised the tunnelling shield for boring through soft ground, and between 1825 and 1843 he used it to construct the Rotherhithe Tunnel under the River Thames.

Thames Tunnel being built

C Canadian, inaugurated in 1955, is one of the great trains of the world. It runs on the Canadian Pacific Railway between Vancouver, Montreal and Toronto. Diesel-hauled throughout the journey of 69 hours 10 minutes, it passes through magnificent scenery and the coaches include an observation lounge with bedrooms.

Cascade Tunnel, on the Great Northern Railway, USA, is the longest tunnel in North America. Opened in 1929, it is 12.542 km long.

Centennial-type locomotives are the most powerful diesel-electric locomotives (6600 hp). From 1969 General Motors Corporation built 47 of these.

Central Railway of Peru reaches the highest altitude of any railway in the world. On a branch line at La Cima it reaches 4,818 metres. On the main line, which reaches a height of 4,781 metres, there are 21 zig-zag reversing stations and the gradient is 1 in 23.

Classification of locomotives is according to the number of wheels or axles. In the Whyte system, steam locomotives are given 3-figure numbers that indicate, in order, the number of front-carrying wheels, the number of driving wheels and the number of rear-carrying wheels. Thus, the 6-wheeled NORTH STAR is classified as 2-2-2 and the 1950s American design, which had a 4-wheeled carrying bogie at the front, four coupled driving wheels and no rear-carrying wheels, is classified as 4-4-0. In the classification

The Railway Revolution

several new ideas and its basic features have been used in all later locomotives. In its original form it could travel at 58 kilometres per hour and it proved its worth by winning the Rainhill trials in 1829. These trials were held by the Liverpool and Manchester Company who were looking for the best locomotive to use on their new railway. In 1830, the Liverpool and Manchester Railway (L&MR) was opened and continued to use locomotives of the *Rocket* type for several years.

The opening of the Liverpool and Manchester Railway is generally thought of as the beginning of the railway age. It was built to compete with existing canals and roads and its success amazed even its builders. The profitability and usefulness of railways being obvious, during the next 90 years over 1,100,000 kilometres of rail were built around the world.

The growth of railways

By 1830 both France and America were using horse-drawn trains and they began experimenting with steam traction by importing a few English-built locomotives. Within a few years, however, both countries were building their own locomotives and developing their own railway systems. After France, other European countries opened steam railways and by 1860 Europe was covered by a network of tracks linking up towns and cities.

In America, the railway era began in 1830 on the Baltimore–Ohio line with the maiden trip of the first American-built locomotive, *Tom Thumb*. As in Britain and Europe tremendous expansion of the railways followed, but in America this had the effect of opening vast new areas of territory. The first trans-continental railway was com-

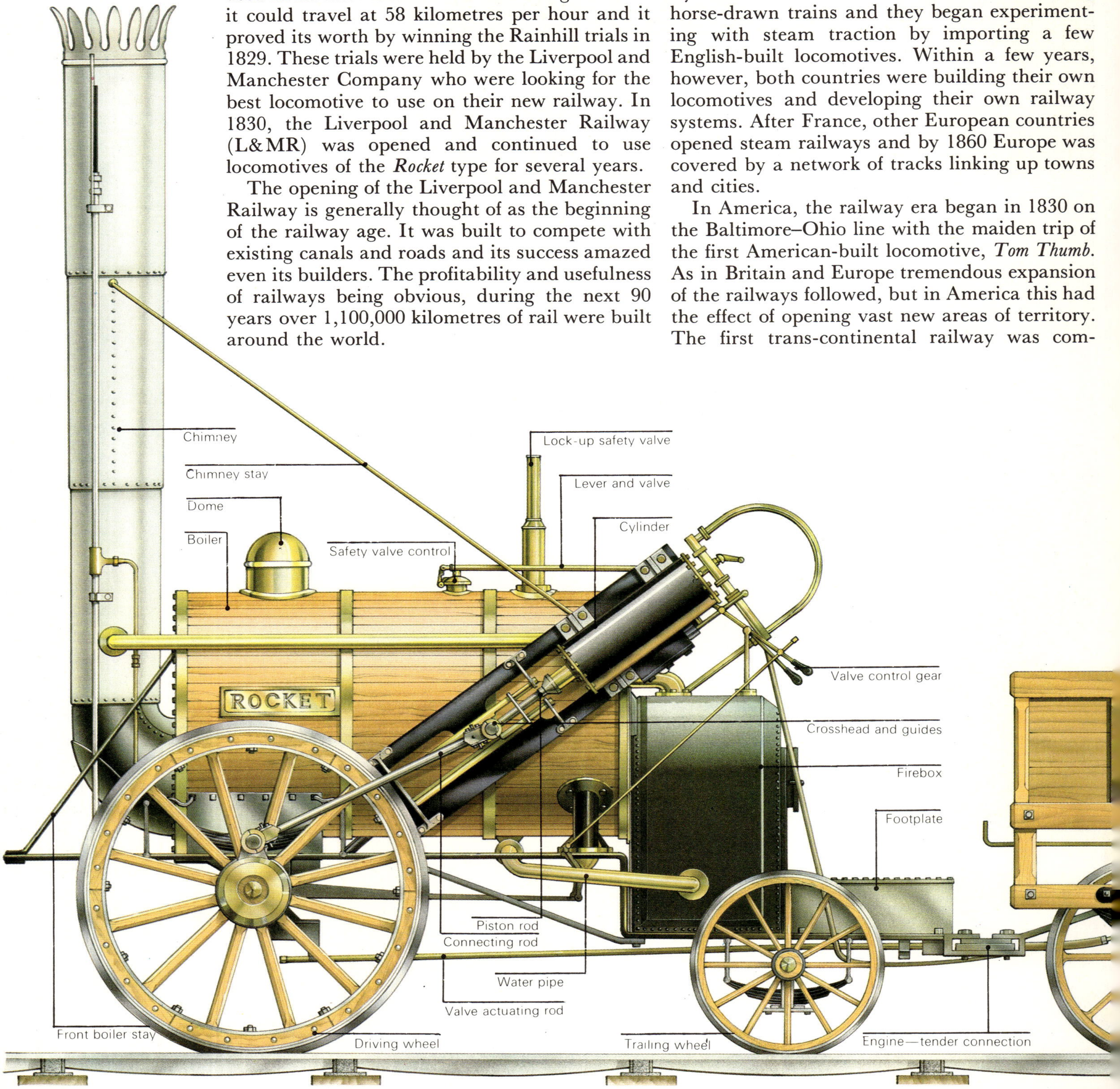

2-6-4T the T indicates a TANK LOCOMOTIVE. In the continental system of classification, which counts axles instead of wheels, these 3 classifications become 1-1-1, 2-2-0 and 1-3-2T. Modern locomotives, particularly diesel and electric, are also classified according to the number of axles, but a system of letters is used to describe the driving axles (A=1, B=2, C=3, D=4, E=5). Thus, a modern 2-D-1 locomotive is equivalent to a 4-8-2 steam locomotive. If the suffix o is used, this indicates that each driving axle is individually driven. A common type is Co-Co.

Couplings, in the early days of railways, were of the chain and hook type. Screw couplings were first used on passenger coaches by the Liverpool and Manchester Railway to eliminate jolting. However, in Britain they were never used on goods wagons. In America the chain and hook couplings were replaced by a rigid link fixed wih a pin. During the 1890s this was superseded by the automatic coupling – a hook that engages a similar hook on the next coach – which later came to be used in Europe as well. In modern coaches automatic couplings now incorporate electrical connections.

Link and pin coupling

D Dead man's handle is a lever in the driving cab of a modern locomotive that the driver has to hold down to keep the train moving. If he becomes incapacitated and releases the handle, the train automatically comes to a halt.

F Festiniog Railway in North Wales was the world's first public narrow-gauge railway (597 mm). It was built to carry wagons loaded with slate from Blaenau Ffestiniog 20.8 km down to Porthmadog. Thus the gradient (averaging 1 in 90) is all 1-way and increases slightly on the curves to prevent heavy trains from sticking. It closed in 1946 and has since been modified

Festiniog Railway

The Railway Revolution

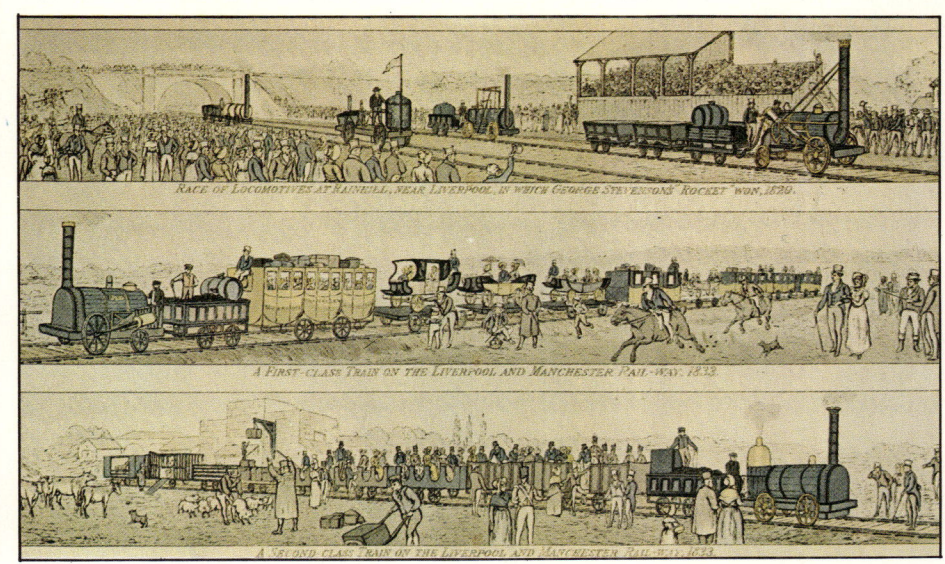

Above: An early railway print showing, at the top, Stephenson's *Rocket* winning the Rainhill trials in 1829. By 1833 first class passengers either travelled in comfortable, stagecoach-style carriages or in their own carriages on top of flat wagons (middle). Second class passengers had to stand in open-topped wagons (bottom).

Left: Stephenson's 1829 *Rocket*, which won the Rainhill trials and opened the Liverpool and Manchester Railway in 1830. One of the main improvements over previous locomotives was the use of inclined cylinders, which enabled a simpler driving gear to be used.

pleted in 1869 with the meeting at Promontory in Utah of the Central Pacific and Grand Union Pacific lines. By 1920, America had 407,000 kilometres of track, Britain had 32,700 kilometres, Germany 11,500 kilometres and France 9,400 kilometres. After 1920, various factors, particularly competition with the increasing amount of road traffic, caused railways to decline, with the result that many lines have since been closed.

In the early days of railways there were many small companies. One of the earliest problems that resulted from this was the use of different GAUGES (the distance between the inner faces of the rails). George Stephenson selected, for no particular reason, a gauge of 1,435 millimetres. However, he had the vision to foresee that all the railways in Britain would eventually link up and saw to it that all the northern lines used this gauge. The great civil engineer Isambard Kingdom BRUNEL, however, was an individualist. He built the Great Western Railway with a gauge of 2,140 millimetres. The advantage of such a broad gauge is that it can carry much heavier loads. On the other hand, narrow-gauge railways are cheaper to build.

When the Great Western and Midland railways met at Gloucester, the 'battle of the gauges' began. Transferring passengers and cargo from one railway to the other was expensive and caused great inconvenience. The government held trials and, although the broad gauge was proved to be the best, there were many more kilometres of the narrower track and in 1846 the Gauge Act standardized Stephenson's 1,435-millimetre gauge.

The Great Western Railway gradually changed its track and by 1892 all of Britain's main railways were using the standard gauge. In France and America it had been adopted from the beginning and so there was no problem. Gauges do vary round the world, however, and there are at present six different standard gauges. The largest of these is 1,676 millimetres and the smallest is 1,000 millimetres.

Wagons and carriages

The original intention of Stephenson and the other railway pioneers was to speed up the transport of coal and other goods. Freight transport is still an important part of railway

to carry tourists uphill as well as down.
Flying Hamburger was the first German high-speed diesel train. From 1933 this twin-unit locomotive hauled trains between Berlin and Hamburg at an average speed of 124 km/hour.
Flying Scotsman is Britain's prestige train. At present it runs between London (King's Cross) and Edinburgh in 5 hours 35 minutes. Originally called the *Special Scottish Express*, it was nicknamed the *Flying Scotsman* during the 1860s. It received the name officially in 1923 and was given Gresley Pacific (4-6-2) locomotives. These were replaced in the 1930s by the streamlined A4 class Pacifics. The train is now hauled by high-powered *Deltic* diesel-electric locomotives.
Forth Railway Bridge, built between 1882 and 1890, is the oldest and second largest cantilever bridge in the world. Its 2 main spans are 520 metres long. With the TAY BRIDGE disaster in mind, the designer spent 2 years conducting wind-pressure tests before it was built. The main struts are tubular.

G Garratt locomotives are ARTICULATED STEAM LOCOMOTIVES. The boiler is carried on a cradle slung between engine units and there are no wheels underneath it. This allows the boiler to be large in diameter and shorter than in the MALLET arrangement. The first Garratts, weighing 32 tonnes, were built in 1908. The largest were the 4-8-4 + 4-8-4 Beyer Garratts, weighing 256 tonnes built for New South Wales Railways in 1952.
Gauge is the distance between the inside faces of the rails. The 6 principal standard gauges in use around the world are 1,676 mm, 1,600 mm, 1,524 mm, 1,435 mm, 1,067 mm and 1,000

Mixed-gauge points system

mm. Today the 1,435-mm gauge is used in many countries including Britain, North America, China, Japan, Australia, Mexico and most of Europe. Some countries have more than one gauge. For example, Switzerland has 3,518 km of 1,435-mm track and 1,183 km of 1,000-mm track; and Argentina has 23,235 km of 1,676-mm track, 3,086 km of 1,435-mm track and 13,461 km of 1,000-mm track. In addition there are various narrow-gauge railways around the world, ranging from 597-mm to 914-mm gauges.

The Railway Revolution

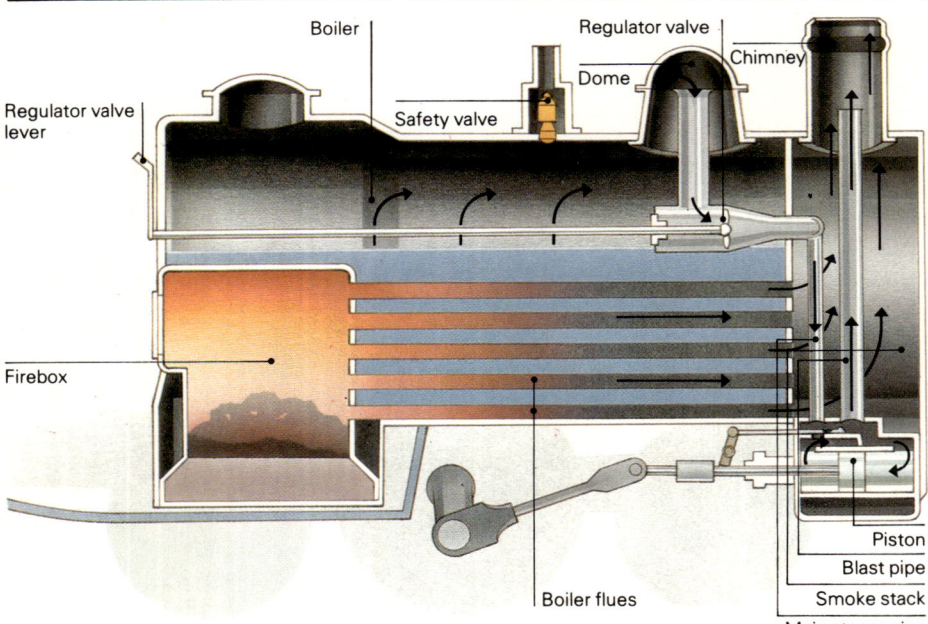

Above: A steam engine. Hot air from the firebox passes down the flues and steam is raised in the boiler. The steam passes via the regulator valve to the cylinders. Valves allow the steam to pass first to one side of the piston and then the other.

Below: *Der Adler* (The Eagle) was built by Robert Stephenson. On December 7 1835 it opened the first German railway, from Nüremberg to Fürth.

operation, but there has been considerable technological improvement. Due to improved suspension systems wagons can now travel much faster and there are many wagons specially designed to carry particular kinds of freight.

The Liverpool and Manchester Railway was the first steam railway to begin a regular passenger service and the first carriages were simply stagecoaches on flanged wheels. Soon, larger carriages were being constructed by placing two or three stagecoach bodies on a single chassis. In Europe, open-topped wagons were introduced as a form of cheap-fare passenger carriage.

The modern style of coach was developed in America, where the early railways often had sharper curves than in Europe. Instead of a short coach set on a single chassis they began to use a long coach on independent trucks, or bogies. The coach could move on central pivots on the bogies and so negotiate sharp corners more easily.

The interiors of coaches have either followed the American open-plan arrangement with a central gangway or the European type with separate, isolated compartments. The first luxury PULLMAN parlour and sleeping cars were introduced in America in the 1860s. But in Europe, and particularly in Britain, it was some time before passenger comfort, below the level of first class, was given much attention. By the 1870s, public pressure had forced the companies to give up some of their precious passenger space (and hence revenue) for lavatories and, later, corridors so that everyone had access to them.

The age of steam locomotives

The principle on which a steam locomotive works is very simple. Burning fuel in the firebox heats water in the boiler and produces steam. This passes to each cylinder and VALVES operate to pass steam first to one side of the piston and then the other. From the earliest days, however, modifications have been made to this basic system to improve the performance of locomotives.

One of the most important discoveries was made by Trevithick. In his locomotive *Penydarran* the exhaust steam was pushed out via the chimney. Each blast of the exhaust created a partial vacuum in the chimney and helped to draw the fire through the boiler flue. All subsequent steam locomotives used this effect

Hell **Gate Bridge**, which carries the Pennsylvania Railroad to Long Island, New York, is the largest steel arch bridge in the USA. Its main span is 297.8 metres long and carries four tracks.
Hero (born *c.* AD 20) was a Greek engineer who lived during the last years of the age of Greek science. In addition to inventing his 'steam engine' he extended the work of Archimedes on levers and constructed gears.
Huey P. Long Bridge across the Mississippi River near New Orleans is the longest railway bridge in the world. Opened in 1935 it is 7.009 km long and has 8 river spans, the longest of which is 241 metres. The bridge also carries road traffic.

The Indian Pacific *passenger express*

Indian **Pacific** is Australia's great train that runs from Perth on the shore of the Indian Ocean to Sydney on the shore of the Pacific Ocean. Diesel-hauled for most of the time, the train travels at a moderate speed and the journey takes 65 hours 45 minutes. On the Nullarbor Plain in Western Australia the Indian Pacific runs on the world's longest pieces of continuous straight track (478 km).

Kanmon **Tunnel** between Honshu and Kyushu on the extension of the SHINKANSEN line in Japan is the longest underwater tunnel in the world. It was completed in 1974 and is 18.7 km long.
Key West Extension, completed in 1912, was built to extend the Florida East Coast Railway 182 km into the sea, with the object of shortening the sea passage to Cuba. Most of the track (135.5 km) is laid on coral reefs called keys. The remainder is built on 27.5 km of bridging and 32 km of embankment. Damaged by a hurricane in 1936, it is now only open to road traffic.

and, later, a steam blower was placed in the chimney to keep the fire drawing when the locomotive was stationary.

In *Locomotion,* Stephenson used a single, straight-through flue. In 1827, Henry Booth, Secretary of the Liverpool and Manchester Company, patented the multi-tubular boiler, which Stephenson incorporated into the *Rocket.* Instead of a single flue running through the boiler, locomotives now had a number of small tubes. This provided a much greater steam-raising capacity. Much later, in the early 1900s, a system of SUPERHEATING was developed. In this system, the steam is passed through small pipes in superheater flues in the upper part of the boiler. It is then delivered to the cylinders at a much higher temperature and has a much greater power of expansion.

All the early locomotives were built with vertical cylinders and the driving wheels were turned by gears. Stephenson's *Rocket,* however, used direct drive from the pistons on to crankpins on the wheels and the cylinders were at an angle of about 45°. By 1850, the design of locomotives had changed considerably. Locomotives like the 2-2-2 NORTH STAR, built by George Stephenson's son Robert, had a single pair of

Above right: Tank engine No. 1247 near New Bridge on the North York Moors Railway in England. Built in 1899, this 0-6-2T locomotive was the first British Rail steam engine to be preserved.

Right: A typical American train of the mid-1800s. The 4-4-0 engine was woodburning, hence the enormous, spark-arresting chimney. The carriages were of the open-plan type with central corridors and they were carried on 2 4-wheel bogies.

Kicking Horse Pass on the Canadian Pacific Railway originally had a gradient of 1 in 23. In 1920 the track was relaid and 2 spiral tunnels were constructed. The gradient was thus reduced to 1 in 45 and more heavily loaded trains could be hauled over the pass at less cost.

King George V, the Great Western Railway locomotive No. 6000, was built by G. J. Churchward and made its first public appearance in 1927 at the Iron Horse Centennial in America. This type of locomotive was one of the few 4-6-0 designs that was a noticeable improvement on the 4-4-0s. After steam had been phased out from British railways, *King George V* was loaned to H. P. Bulmer, the cider makers of Hereford, to haul an exhibition train in 1968 and is now preserved at their railway centre. On March 2 1979 this now-famous locomotive hauled a train from Paddington to Didcot to celebrate the 125th anniversary of Paddington Station. Unfortunately, an overheated axlebox prevented it from making the return journey.

Linear electric motor is one that produces motion in a straight line instead of a rotary motion. Only prototype linear motors have yet been built and they are mostly linear induction motors. Such a motor consists of a moving body containing coils and a stationary track formed from a metal strip. Electric current passed through the coils creates a magnetic field that travels in a straight line and the effect of this is to propel the moving body along the track.

Locomotion was the locomotive built by George STEPHENSON for the opening of the Stockton and Darling-

The Locomotion, *c.1890*

ton Railway. It was similar to earlier locomotives in that it still had vertical cylinders which were set into the top of the boiler. However, it was one of the first to have outside coupling rods on the wheels.

Lower Zambezi Bridge in Mozambique is the second longest railway bridge in the world. A steel truss bridge, it is 3.677 km long and has 33 main spans of 7.9 metres each.

Magnetic levitation (MAGLEV) is one of the ways in which a hovertrain

The Railway Revolution

driving wheels and four carrying wheels. The American 4-4-0 design (*see* CLASSIFICATION) had a four-wheeled bogie at the front and four driving wheels. This long wheel-base design rode better on the American tracks, which were rougher than British tracks. In Britain, the long boiler design began to develop. The smokeboxes of short-boilered locomotives tended to overheat, whereas in long-boilered locomotives more heat was absorbed along the fire tubes.

The early American locomotives burned wood and their vast funnel-shaped chimneys were designed to prevent sparks from flying out. Other well-known features of such locomotives included the large lamp for lighting up the track at night and the cowcatcher, which was necessary for sweeping away branches and other obstacles.

In Britain, the first locomotives burned coal. However, they emitted large quantities of dirty black smoke and for several years coke was used instead. In about 1860 the idea of a brick arch in the firebox was developed. This improved the combustion of the fuel, and coal, much cheaper than coke, could once again be used.

At about the same time steel came into use. Boilers built of steel could withstand higher steam pressures and locomotives became larger and more powerful. During the late 1800s the compound engine was introduced. In this type of engine, steam is used first in a high-pressure cylinder and then allowed to expand in a larger low-pressure cylinder. Compound engines use less fuel and water and were popular in Europe.

In the late 1800s and early 1900s even larger locomotives were built. In Britain the outstanding 4-4-0s appeared, followed by the 4-4-2s (Atlantics) which were a great success on long-distance express routes. In America the 4-4-2s were followed by the great 4-6-2s (Pacifics), 4-6-4s (Hudsons) and 4-8-4s. The largest locomotives of all were the articulated MALLETS and GARRATTS, built for hauling heavy trains up steep slopes. The largest locomotive ever built was the UNION PACIFIC BIG BOY 4-8-8-4.

Over the years a vast number of different types of locomotive were built for different tasks and engineers were constantly trying to build better locomotives. However, by the 1940s the end of the age of steam was in sight. The 4-6-0 MALLARD still holds the world speed record for a steam locomotive (202 kilometres per hour). However, many steam locomotives are in use in various parts of the world and even where diesel and electric traction have superseded steam many locomotives have been preserved by enthusiasts.

Modern locomotives

The first diesel-electric locomotives appeared in 1924 and today most so-called diesel locomotives are of this type. Their engines power generators which provide electricity for the electric traction motors that turn the wheels. A few diesel-mechanical locomotives exist, together with a few diesel-hydraulic locomotives which use a system similar to that of a motor car with AUTOMATIC TRANSMISSION (*see page 17*).

Unlike steam locomotives, the basic design of diesel-electric locomotives is much the same all over the world. After a few initial experiments it was found that the best arrangement was to mount the body on two independent bogies and to power the driving axles separately.

Diesel-electric locomotives are more efficient than steam locomotives and can go further without refuelling or servicing. In addition, they are easy to use as multiple units and this is particularly useful in America, where as many as

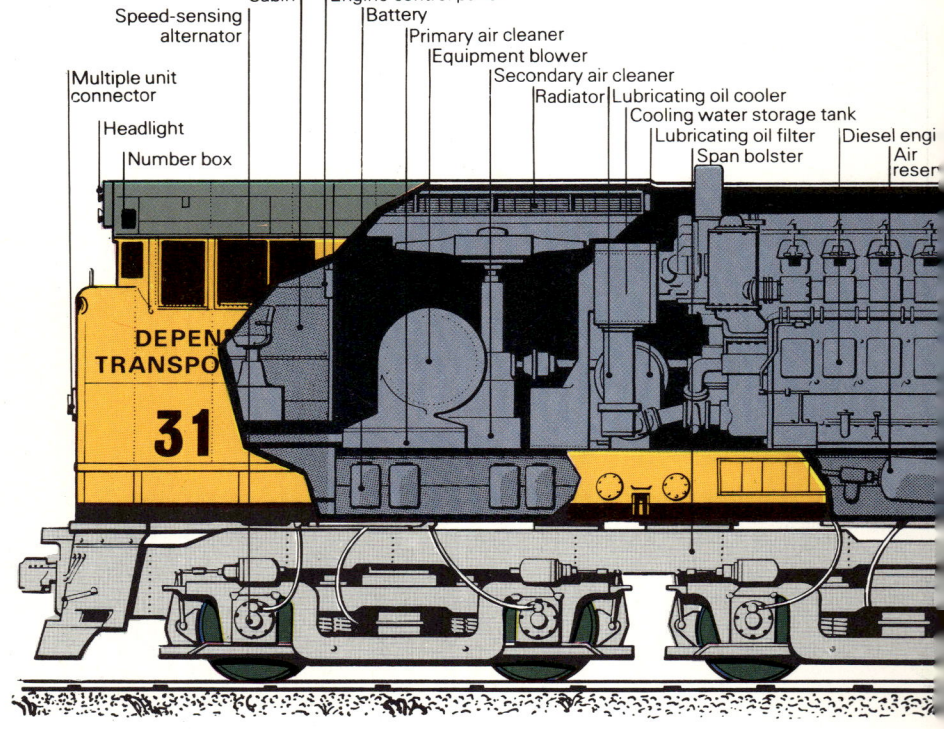

Below: A cutaway of a Do-Do General Electric 5,000 hp diesel-electric locomotive. The diesel engines are used to turn the traction generator which keeps the batteries charged. Electric current from the batteries powers the traction motors, which are linked to the axles by gears.

---

might be raised off its track. The principle used is the repulsion effect between 2 strong magnetic fields created by electromagnets in the train and on the track.
Mallard is the streamlined A4 class Gresley Pacific locomotive No. 4468 that holds the recognized world speed record for a steam locomotive. On July 3 1938 it achieved a speed of 202 km/hour down Stoke Bank near Peterborough in England. The engine was severely damaged.
Mallet locomotives were ARTICULATED STEAM LOCOMOTIVES. The earliest type, which appeared in 1889, was a compound locomotive, with the rear end of the boiler fixed to the rear chassis. The largest compound Mallets were the 2-10-10-2s built in America in the 1920s. Later Mallets were simple-expansion locomotives. They had very long, narrow boilers. The largest type was UNION PACIFIC BIG BOY 4-8-8-4.
Marsh, Sylvester (1803–84), an American entrepreneur, built the first mountain rack railway, the Mount Washington Cog Railway, in 1868. He used a ladder rack system with round bars.
Mistral is the train that runs from Paris to Nice on the French Riviera. It earned the name because the 4-4-0 locomotives that pulled the train during the late 1880s had an early form of streamlining to combat the terrific Mistral wind that sweeps down from the Maritime Alps. The Mistral has always been a high-speed train and today the electric locomotives average 121.5 km/hour and in places reach 160 km/hour. The journey takes 6 hours 51 minutes.
Mont Cenis Tunnel (Fréjus Tunnel) was the first of the major tunnels bored through the Alps. Work began in 1857 and it took 14 years to build. The 14-km tunnel was bored from both ends and ventilation problems were solved by using water-powered fans and a horizontal diaphragm that divided off the upper part of the tunnel as an exhaust duct.
N Newcomen, Thomas (1663–1729) was an English engineer. In 1698 he went into partnership with

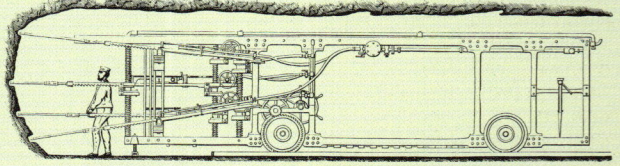

Sommellier drilling machine, Mont Cenis Tunnel, 1871

The Railway Revolution 41

Above: A massive 2-10-2 freight locomotive in a coal yard in China.

Right: The A3 class Gresley Pacific (4-6-2) No. 4472 was the first to be named *Flying Scotsman.* Built in the 1920s, it has since been restored.

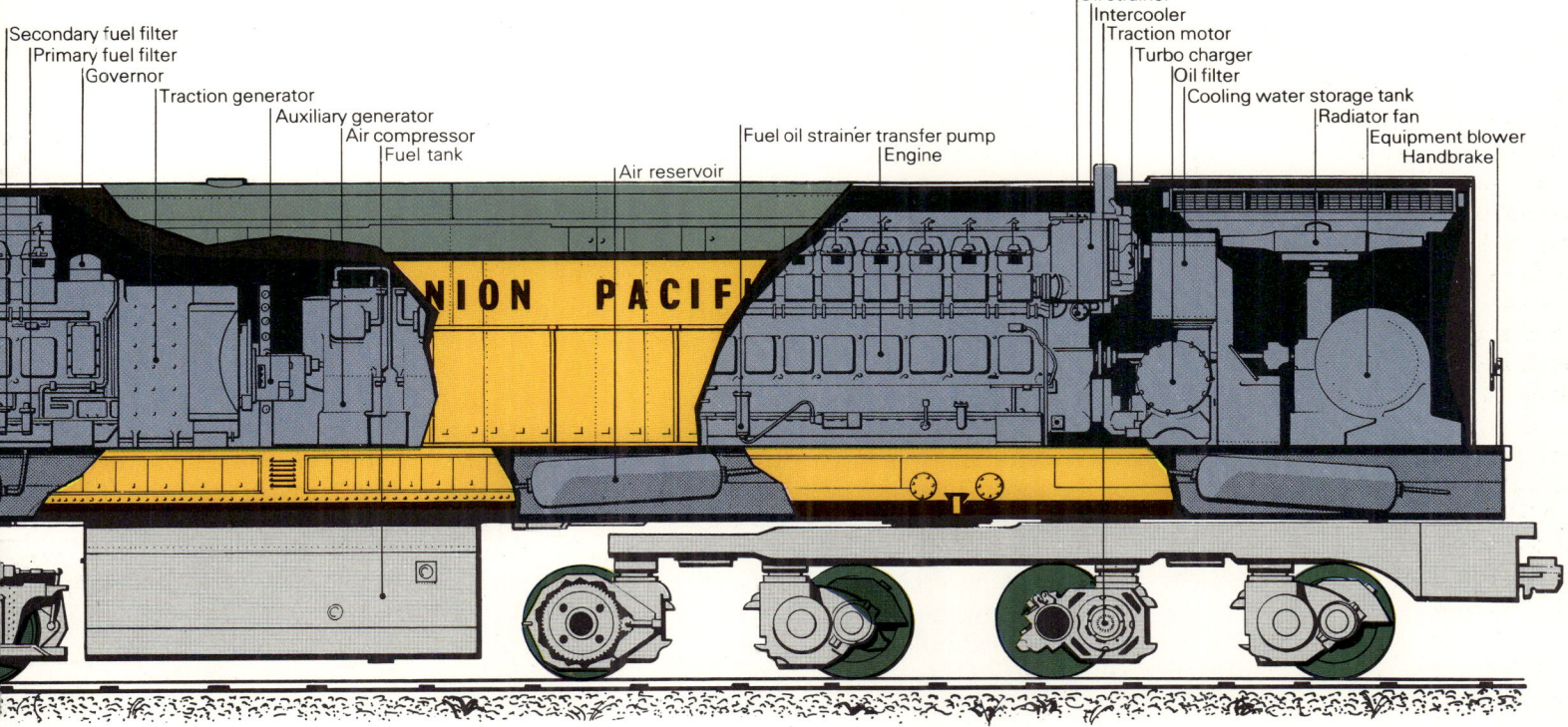

SAVERY. He built an improved steam engine and to do this he had to construct highly polished cylinders into which pistons would fit to form an air-tight seal.

Northern Line on London's underground railway is the longest continuous tunnel in the world (27.8 km).

North Star was the 2-2-2 locomotive built in 1837 by Robert STEPHENSON for the broad-gauge Great Western Railway. It hauled the first train on this line in 1838 and remained Great Western Railway's best locomotive for several years.

O Orient Express is the famous train that ran from Paris to Constantinople (now Istanbul). The service from Paris to Vienna, Budapest, Bucharest and Varna on the Black Sea was inaugurated in 1883 and the link to Constantinople was completed by boat. In 1889, the route from Budapest was changed and the whole journey, now via Belgrade, was completed by train in 67 hours 35 minutes. When the SIMPLON TUNNEL was opened in 1906 a rival service was introduced. Today, the *Orient Express* runs from Paris to Vienna and Budapest, with through carriages to Bucharest four days a week. The *Simplon Orient,* now called the *Direct Orient,* runs from Paris to Belgrade via Lausanne, Milan, Venice and Trieste; through services are provided to the cities of Istanbul and Athens by the *Marmara* and the *Athens Express*.

P Papin, Denis (1647–1712) was a French physicist. In 1769 he developed a steam digester – the forerunner of the modern pressure cooker – and went on to experiment with steam engines.

Penydarran was Richard TREVITHICK's second locomotive, built in 1804. It could haul about 25 tonnes and climb a 1 in 36 gradient. Its horizontal boiler had a U-shaped flue and a single cylinder drove the wheels on one side by means of a system of gears.

Pilatus Railway in Switzerland is the steepest rack railway in the world – in places 1 in 2. The carriages are stepped and the railway uses the Locher rack system, in which a pair of horizontal

Mount Pilatus Railway

The Railway Revolution

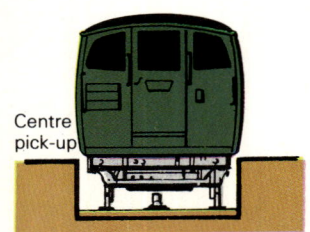

Above: Electric trains often receive their current from a third rail, which runs either in between the two carrying rails (top) or to one side (bottom).

Left: An electric train on the Rhaetian Railway in Switzerland showing the pantograph that collects current from overhead wires. The pantograph is spring-loaded, so that it always follows the contours of the wire, and it can be retracted.

Right: The cab of a modern diesel-electric locomotive. The controls are easier to handle than those of a steam locomotive, but the driver still needs a high degree of concentration.

five diesel-electric units may be used to pull the heaviest trains.

The first electric locomotives were built in the 1830s, but until the 1880s they were powered by batteries, which were heavy and needed recharging at frequent intervals. In 1883, the first true electric railway was built by Magnus Volk in Brighton and this railway still operates as a tourist attraction along the sea front. Electric current is collected from a third rail.

One of the most important applications of electric traction is in underground railways. In England, the first section of the Metropolitan railway had been opened in 1863, but steam trains were used, with the result that the tunnels filled with smoke. After 1890 electric locomotives were brought into use on the line between the City of London and Stockwell.

Today, many electric trains are multiple units in which a number of individually-propelled coaches can be controlled by a single driver from either end of the train. The system was invented by the American Frank Sprague in 1897. Sprague had also invented the swivel trolley pole in 1888 for the Union Passenger Railway in Virginia and this led to the modern pantograph which collects current from overhead wires.

Electric trains have several advantages. They are clean, accelerate rapidly (especially multiple-unit trains) and can climb gradients more easily than steam or diesel locomotives. However, they are not cheap to run and the cost of electrification is enormous.

Monorails

In 1824, a wooden monorail was built in England between the Royal Victualling Yard and the River Thames to carry horse-drawn trains. During the late 1800s several trestle railways were built, the last of which was the Listowel to Ballybunion line in Ireland, which ran from 1887 to 1924. The train was supported on a central rail about a metre from the ground. On either side of the trestles which supported the central rail were guide rails. The locomotive and carriages were divided into two, with the wheels in the middle.

Between 1903 and 1910 a series of monorails were built on which the trains were guided and kept upright by gyroscopes. A more successful system is that on the Wuppertal Railway in Germany, which has been in use since 1901. There the cars are suspended from a single line of wheels running on an overhead rail. Another successful monorail was invented by the Swedish industrialist Dr Axel L. Wenner-Gren. In this Alweg system, the cars straddle a central beam on which they are driven by rubber-tyred wheels. There are four rows of wheels (two on each side)

---

pinions grip a central rail that has teeth on both sides. The Pilatus Railway was opened in 1889 and electrified in 1937.
Puffing Billy was built in 1814 by William Hedley (1779–1843), who also built *Wylam Billy* and *Lady Mary*. These 3 locomotives had boilers like those of Trevithick locomotives and their 2 cylinders drove the wheels through a system of rods, cranks and gears. They travelled at walking pace and hauled loads of about 50 tonnes. All 3 locomotives had long lives. *Puffing Billy* was still in use in 1859 and is now preserved in the Science Museum in London.
Pullman, George (1831–97) was the founder of the Pullman Car Company. In Chicago in 1858 he rebuilt 2 coaches into sleeping cars and in 1865 he built the first Pullman Car. He founded his company in 1867 and introduced dining cars (1868), chaircars (1875) and vestibule cars (1887).

R Re 6/6 electric Bo-Bo-Bo locomotives, built in Switzerland from 1972, are the world's most powerful electric locomotives. Weighing 122 tonnes, they produce 10,450 hp and can travel at 140 km/hour.
Rhaetian Railway in Switzerland uses 4 spiral tunnels to reach the mountain valley tourist resort of St Moritz. At one point 1 of the tunnels is vertically above another This railway also uses snow galleries to prevent the line being covered by avalanches, and magnificent masonry viaducts. The Landwasser viaduct carries the line from a tunnel entrance in a vertical cliff face. It has a gradient of 1 in 29 and is built in a series of angles so that it appears to curve.
Riggenbach, Nikolaus (1817–95) was experimenting with rack railways at the same time as MARSH. He patented his ladder-rack in 1863 and used it on the Kahlenberg Railway near Vienna, which opened in 1874. It is generally held that the bars of Riggenbach's ladder were better shaped to mesh with the pinion than those of Marsh's ladder.
Rocket was the STEPHENSON locomotive that won the Rainhill trials in 1829 and opened the Liverpool and

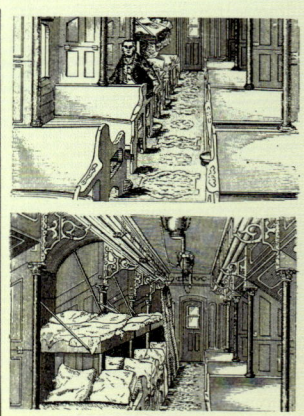

Pullman sleeping car, 1880

The Railway Revolution

that support and guide the cars. The Tokyo–Haneda Airport railway is an Alweg monorail that has run successfully since 1964.

Above: The Snowdon Mountain Railway, opened in 1896, is a tourist line that uses the double Abt rack system. It is Britain's highest railway and climbs to a height of 1,064 metres.

Below: The electric Wuppertal monorail that runs along the valley between Barmen and Elberfeld in West Germany. It is 13 km long and for most of the way runs over the River Wupper.

Mountain railways

In the early 1800s trains were hauled up steep inclines by stationary engines. From this developed the idea of self-acting cableways on which loaded descending wagons hauled up empty wagons. Today, much the same principle is used on funicular railways. A descending coach attached to one end of a cable is balanced by an ascending coach attached to the other end. Such railways are generally single-track, with a short double-track section where the coaches pass each other.

However, engineers wanted a system by which a locomotive could move up a steep slope under its own power. The Fell system, first used across the Mont Cenis pass in 1868, had two extra horizontal wheels that gripped a central rail. However, rack railways have proved to be the best for negotiating steep slopes.

The first rack railway was built in 1812 by John Blenkinsop. Alongside one of the rails he laid an additional toothed rail, or rack, which meshed with a cog, or pinion, on the locomotive. In 1874, Nikolaus RIGGENBACH built a mountain railway in Austria. His rack was a ladder of bars

Manchester Railway in 1830. It had the first multitubular boiler and an external firebox with a water-jacketed top and sides. The 2 upturned exhaust steam nozzles in the smokestack had constrictions at their ends to intensify the action of the exhaust blast in drawing the fire. Its 2 outside cylinders were inclined and there was direct drive on to the wheels. In its original form it had a top speed of 58 km/hour; when the cylinders were lowered, the top speed was increased to 80 km/hour.

Royal George, built by Timothy Hackworth in 1827, was the first 6-coupled (0-6-0) locomotive and the first to have direct drive on to the wheels.

S St Gotthard Tunnel is one of the major tunnels through the Alps. It is 14.99 km long and was bored between 1872 and 1882. The builders had great problems with weak rock and water inflows.

Savery, Thomas (1650–1715) was a prolific English inventor. His most important invention was the Miner's Friend, a form of steam pump for removing water from coal mines.

Severn Tunnel is the longest tunnel in Britain (7.011 km) and when it was completed in 1886 it was the longest

St Gotthard Tunnel

underwater tunnel in the world. It was built by Sir John Hawkshaw for the Great Western Railway extension to South Wales. During construction a tremendous inflow of water from the Great Spring was encountered and a massive steam pump was used to remove 7 million litres of water an hour.

Shinkansen Hikari are the Japanese 'lightning trains' that run every 15 minutes between Tokyo and Osaka. A new line was specially built for the service, which was inaugurated in 1964, and the bullet-nosed, multiple-unit electric trains travel at about 210 km/hour nearly all the way. In 1975 the line was extended to the island of Kyushu in the south and the new track was built to take trains travelling at 260 km/hour. The extension included 222 km of tunnels, one of which was the KANMON TUNNEL, and 117 km of bridges and viaducts.

Siemens, Dr Ernst Werner von (1816–92) built the first electric railway at the Berlin Trades Exhibition in 1879. The 550-metre line was straight and level and the

The Railway Revolution

Above: The fine vaulted roof over the platforms of St Pancras Station in London. The station is a classic example of Victorian Gothic architecture. It was designed in 1865 by Sir George Scott and was opened in 1866.

Middle: Massive marble pillars support the roof of this station on the Moscow Underground system.

Bottom: A wooden trestle bridge built in 1900 on the Northern Pacific Railway, between Cul-de-Sac and Grangeville, Idaho, in America. The photograph was taken in 1910 and the bridge has since been replaced with a steel structure.

shaped to mesh with the pinion. The rack invented by Roman ABT is today the most popular. It consists of a single-toothed rail that meshes closely with the pinion. First used in 1886 on the Blankenburg Railway in Brunswick, it is now used in many parts of the world. Many railways, such as the Snowdon Mountain Railway in Wales, use a double Abt rack system. This has two racks and the teeth of one are staggered in relation to the teeth of the other. A special rack system was devised by Colonel Locher-Freuler for the very steep railway (1 in 2, in places) at PILATUS in Switzerland. The rack rail has teeth on each side that mesh with a pair of pinions.

In the early days of rack railways, engineers realized that the boiler of a conventional steam locomotive would dry out at one end when the train was on a gradient. At first, vertical boilers were used to overcome this problem, but engineers soon began to build locomotives that appeared tilted on the flat but were horizontal on the gradient. Today many rack railways are electrified.

Railway engineering

Railway tracks, except those on mountain railways, need to be as level and as straight as possible to reduce the cost of working the railway. When building a railway, the final choice of route depends on balancing this cost against the cost of construction. Generally railways tend to go through cuttings and tunnels rather than round or over obstacles, and high bridges are often needed to cross rivers and valleys.

One form of tunnel construction is called 'cut and cover'. A trench is dug, lined, and then covered over. This method was used to build London's Metropolitan and Circle lines. However, deeper tunnels have to be bored. In the early days of railways, hard rock was tunnelled using explosives and tools. In 1861 Germain Sommeiller, while digging the MONT CENIS TUNNEL, invented the pneumatic (compressed air) drill, which made tunnelling somewhat faster. Soft ground was very difficult to tunnel until the invention of the tunnelling shield by Marc Isambard BRUNEL in 1818. As the shield moved forward, cutting into the ground, the brick lining to the tunnel was built behind it.

---

small, 3-hp locomotive collected current from a central third rail.

Signals, in the early days, were simple, 2-aspect semaphore signals that indicated 'stop' or 'proceed'. Later, an additional 2-aspect signal that indicated 'proceed with caution' or 'proceed at full speed' was introduced. As railways became busier, signals came closer together and these 2 kinds of signal were combined into 3-aspect signals, each with 2 semaphore arms. Today nearly all signals are coloured lights, visible in daylight. Four-aspect signals were introduced to control both fast and slow trains. On such signals a red light indicates 'stop', a green light indicates 'proceed at full speed' and a single amber light indicates 'proceed with caution' to all trains. However, a double amber light gives fast trains (over 110 km/hour) advance warning of an approaching 'caution' signal and gives them time to slow down; slower trains may proceed at full speed past a double amber light. At busy junctions there used to be large gantries of semaphore signals. These have now been replaced by single sets of lights with illuminated indicators.

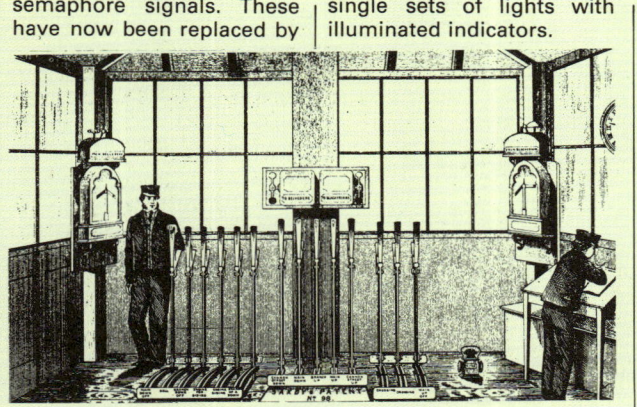

Signal box at Waterloo, England, 1865

Simplon Tunnels are the longest tunnels through the Alps. The first was bored between 1898 and 1906 and is 19.803 km long. It is a single track tunnel with a passing place in the middle. The second tunnel, completed in 1922, is 19.823 km long and, excluding London Transport's NORTHERN LINE, is the longest in the world.

Speed on the railways is increasing all the time. The current records for the various forms of propulsion are: steam – *Mallard*, 1938 – 202 km/hour; electric – French Co-Co No. 7107, 1955 – 330

The Railway Revolution 45

Left: In mountainous country railway lines often have to follow tortuous paths to avoid steep gradients. Here, at Georgetown, USA, in order to raise the line through about 15 metres, engineers have had to construct a loop and two bridges.

Below: Sydney Harbour Bridge is one of the most famous bridges in the world. Its steel arch weighs 39,000 tonnes.

Later, a compressed air chamber was added behind the shield, and today prefabricated cast-iron or concrete sections are used instead of bricks to line tunnels.

Tunnelling is still expensive, difficult and often dangerous. Hazards that may occur, particularly in deep, hard-rock tunnels, include inrushes of water from underground springs and the occurrence of weak rock strata deep inside mountains. In long tunnels, there is the problem of ventilation, sometimes solved by driving long shafts down from the surface above.

In order to avoid long detours and to take the weight of trains, railway builders had to build bridges larger and stronger than ever before. Over long spans, ordinary beam bridges were not strong enough and between 1845 and 1850 Robert STEPHENSON built the first iron box-girder bridge, the BRITANNIA BRIDGE, across the Menai Straits in Wales. In America, where wood was cheap and easily available, many timber trestle bridges were built. Arch bridges have also been successful in all parts of the world, including solidly-built stone viaducts and long-span steel arches. However, the most massive railway bridges are the great cantilever bridges, notably the FORTH RAILWAY BRIDGE in Scotland. Suspension bridges are mostly built for road traffic as they are not suitable for withstanding the heavy loads and vibration on railways.

km/hour; diesel – British Rail HST prototype, 1973 – 230 km/hour; gas turbine (rail) – British Rail experimental APT, 1975 – 244 km/hour; gas turbine (hovertrain) – French *Aerotrain*, 1967 – 378 km/hour; linear induction motor test vehicle (USA), 1974 – 410 km/hour.
Stephenson, George (1781–1841) was an English inventor. His father was the fireman for a steam engine used to pump water out of a coal mine and he became fascinated by machines. He invented a miner's lamp (at about the same time as Sir Humphry Davy) and studied the work of WATT. He set out to devise a travelling steam engine, and although he was not the first to achieve this (see TREVITHICK) his machines were so successful that he is often regarded as the 'inventor' of the steam locomotive. Stephenson was also a great railway engineer and after 1825 concentrated mostly on building railways.
Stephenson, Robert (1803–59) was the son of George STEPHENSON and one of the greatest early railway engineers. He assisted his father in surveying for the Stockton and Darlington Railway and took over the management of Robert Stephenson and Company

Robert Stephenson

in 1823. After spending some time in Colombia, he returned to help his father build the *Rocket* and was appointed engineer of the London and Birmingham Railway in 1838. He built several great bridges, including the BRITANNIA BRIDGE, and a number of successful locomotives.
Superheating is a method of increasing the temperature of steam after it leaves the boiler barrel via the regulator valve. It passes to a saturated steam header which leads to a number of small superheating tubes. Each tube is located within a superheater flue in the boiler and is folded so that the steam makes 4 passes down the flue. The superheated steam is then passed to the cylinders via the superheated steam header and the VALVES.
Sydney Harbour Bridge, built between 1924 and 1932, is perhaps the greatest steel arch bridge in the world because of its load-carrying capacity. Its main span is 503 metres long and carries 4 rail tracks, a roadway and 2 pedestrian walkways. The arch was erected

The Railway Revolution

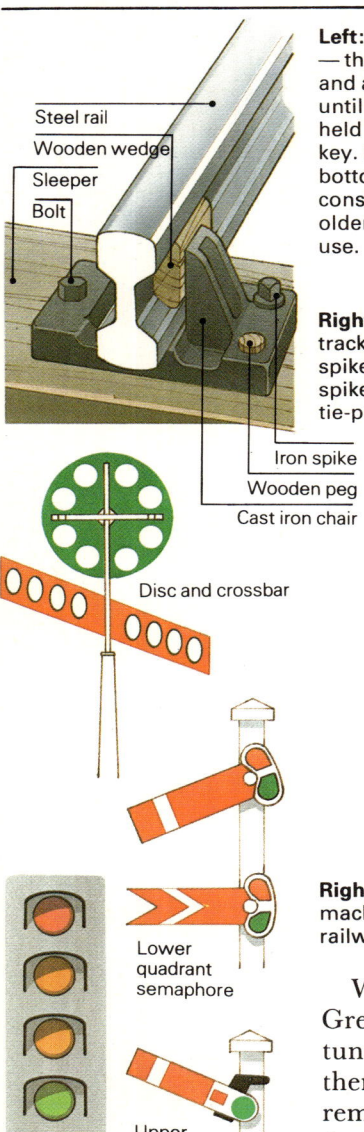

A chaired bullhead rail — the type used in Britain and a few other countries until the 1950s. The rail is held in place by a wooden key. Modern rails are flat-bottomed, but a considerable amount of the older type of rail is still in use.

Right, above: Laying new track, using an automatic spikemaster to drive in the spikes that hold down the tie-plates.

Right: A track-aligning machine on Alice Springs railway in Australia.

Above: Early signals were of the 'stop/go' type. The green disc and red crossbar were set at right angles and the signal turned so that the driver could see the appropriate indicator. Later came three-aspect semaphore signals. Both the upper and lower quadrant signals shown here indicate 'proceed with caution'. Most modern signals are colour lights, like the four-aspect signal here.

When Isambard Kingdom Brunel built the Great Western Railway, he designed all the tunnels, bridges and viaducts himself. He built them to last and the Great Western Railway remains a masterpiece of engineering. He also designed Paddington Station at the London end of the line. Built to impress the railway travellers of the time, this and the other great Victorian stations remain as monuments to the early railway builders.

Tracks and signals

When the roadbed, the ground on which the track is to be laid, has been levelled and the tunnels and bridges have been constructed, the track can be laid. On the first railways the rails were laid on stone blocks, but George Stephenson soon began to use wooden cross-ties, or sleepers. Today these are still used, although sometimes they have been replaced by steel or concrete sleepers and in places concrete slab track has been installed instead.

Sleepers are laid on a ballast of sharp stones, which in turn is laid on a bed of sand. The ballast helps to spread the load over a wide area and allows water to drain away from the track. After the sleepers have been laid more ballast is placed around them and then compacted down. Finally the rails are laid over the sleepers. In Britain and a few other countries rails that lie in supports called chairs fixed to the sleepers were used until the 1950s. Today, however, flat-bottomed rails are fixed to the sleepers using tie-plates. The length of rails also varies in different parts of the world. In Europe the standard rail is 30 metres long and in America it is 39 metres. Increasingly, however, track is being laid using continuous welded rail. Lengths up to 300 metres are laid by special trains and then welded together.

As the amount and speed of traffic on the

---

as 2 cantilevers, held back by cables until they met in the middle. Then the hangers and deck were added.

Tank locomotive is one that carries its own water and fuel supplies.

Tay Bridge, opened in 1878 across the Firth of Tay in Scotland, was a wrought iron truss bridge. It had 84 spans and during a gale on the night of December 28 1879 the central 13 spans collapsed while the Edinburgh mail train was crossing. None of the 78 people on board survived. The reason for the disaster was that the bridge had not been braced to withstand high wind pressures. The bridge was rebuilt and completed in 1887. It now has 85 spans and is the longest bridge in Europe (3.552 km).

The Tay Bridge disaster, December 28, 1879

Tees Bridge was a suspension bridge built in about 1830 to carry the Stockton and Darlington Railway across the River Tees. Within a few years it had been hammered to destruction. The weights of trains and the vibration they produce were thus shown to be too much for a flexible suspension bridge.

Tender is a special wagon, coupled more or less permanently to a steam engine, used for carrying fuel and water. Fuel was shovelled into the firebox by the fireman, but at the same time the boiler had to be replenished with water. Some early locomotives had a water pump operated by a wheel axle, with the disadvantage that the locomotive had to be in motion for it to work. Later locomotives used steam, controlled by a valve lever in the driving cab, to inject water into the boiler.

Track circuit is an electrical circuit, connected to SIGNAL lights, in which the rails form part of the circuit. The track is divided into sections, or blocks. A train on the rails of a block short circuits the

railways have increased, the problem of control has become greater. In 1889, semaphore SIGNALS, with coloured lights for night use, came into service on all British railways, and points were mechanically linked to signals to prevent accidents. Signals and points were operated by levers in signal boxes and a system of lever interlocking ensured that the signalman could not set up a route that might result in a collision.

Initially, two-aspect signals were used, but as the spacing between signals decreased three-aspect signals, indicating 'stop', 'caution' or 'proceed at full speed', were introduced. Today coloured lights, first introduced in 1920, are used in many places instead of semaphore signals.

TRACK CIRCUITS use electric currents to detect the presence of a train on the rails. They were first used in 1870 and today play an important part in controlling busy railways. The track is divided into sections and the arrival of a train in one section automatically changes the signals in the sections behind.

Track circuits have also enabled the use of illuminated track diagrams in control centres, which are gradually replacing manual signal boxes. A track diagram shows the positions of all the trains in the area and identifies them by numbers. Motorized points can be operated by buttons on the diagram and the controller can use these to set up a route. Detectors on the points check that they are locked, the route lights up on the diagram to indicate that it is clear and the signals then operate to allow a train to pass.

Electronic control is also of great importance in modern marshalling yards. In the early days, making up a goods train by shunting each wagon into a siding was a laborious and slow business. The introduction of the marshalling yard hump speeded up the process. Loaded wagons could be shunted to the top of the hump and then allowed to roll into the correct siding. Later, power operated points and wagon retarders (braking devices fixed to the tracks) allowed a few men to operate a marshalling yard from a control tower. However, judging how much braking to apply to each wagon was very difficult. Today, all the necessary information, such as the loaded weight of a particular wagon, how freely it rolls, how full the siding is already, and the wind force, is fed into a computer. The controller merely selects the desired classification siding and the wagon is

Above: Controllers at work in a modern signal control centre. The control panels are positioned to give them a clear view of the illuminated track diagram around the wall.

Below: A marshalling yard near Midway, Chicago, in America. Wagons from the hump (out of the picture to the left) are directed to the correct classification sidings by controllers in a tower.

track circuit and the 4-aspect signal immediately behind turns red. On the 3 blocks behind this the electric circuits select, in order, a single amber signal, a double amber signal and a green signal.

Trans-Siberian Express (the *Russia*) is a train that makes the longest journey in the world. Trains run every day and it takes about 8 days to travel the distance of 9,297 km. The original route, completed in 1904, runs from Moscow through Kirov, Sverdlovsk, Omsk, Krasnoyarsk, Irkutsk, Chita, Skovo-rodino and Khabarovsk to Vladivostok. Travellers can use 'hard' cars, in which only seats are provided, 'soft' cars, in which there are 'places for lying', or 'soft first category' cars, which are modern sleeping cars.

Trevithick, Richard (1771–1883) was the inventor of the high-pressure steam engine. He built 2 steam carriages and 4 steam locomotives. However, although his locomotives worked well he had a great deal of bad luck and had to contend with broken axles, fires and public hostility. He began the Rotherhithe Tunnel, but had to abandon the work and it was later built by Marc BRUNEL. He went to Peru, where he built 9 mine engines. But in order

Trevithick's Common Road Passenger locomotive, 1803

to return home he had to borrow money from Robert STEPHENSON, who was also in South America at the time. Trevithick died in poverty, having failed to obtain any recompense for his many ideas and achievements.

U Union Pacific Big Boys were the largest locomotives ever built. They were 4-8-8-4 MALLETS and 25 were built by the American Locomotive Company between 1941 and 1944. They weighed about 350 tonnes and the total weight, with

The Railway Revolution

Left: A Japanese Hikari bullet-train crossing a steel truss bridge at high speed. Mount Fuji San is in the background.

Above: British Rail's Advanced Passenger train taking a curve at high speed. Its 'pendulum' suspension system causes it to tilt inwards to a greater degree than a conventional train, thus maintaining passenger comfort as well as safety.

slowed down by exactly the right amount to allow it to join the end of the train. Some marshalling yards even do without controllers. Electronic sensing devices 'read' colour codes on the sides of the wagons, which are then automatically directed into the correct siding.

Railways today

There are at present about 1,223,000 kilometres of track around the world and railways provide an increasingly important service. In the last few years railway planners have concentrated to a large extent on high-speed travel. Fast trains now run between major cities in many countries. British Rail's high-speed trains can reach speeds of up to 200 kilometres per hour. In Japan, the bullet trains that run on the SHINKANSEN line can achieve speeds of 210 kilometres per hour. However, above these speeds conventional trains cause discomfort to passengers when going round curves. The solution to this problem has been found by the builders of the gas-turbine-powered British Advanced Passenger Train. With its new 'pendulum' suspension system it will be able to negotiate curves at speeds of up to 240 kilometres per hour. Even this may not be the limit. In the future hovertrains may be built. They will have no wheels but will be raised off their tracks by air-cushions (*see page 62*) or MAGNETIC LEVITATION and may be propelled by LINEAR ELECTRIC MOTORS. Such trains may reach speeds of up to 480 kilometres per hour.

Below: The British Rail MAGLEV (magnetic levitation) test vehicle on its short length of track.

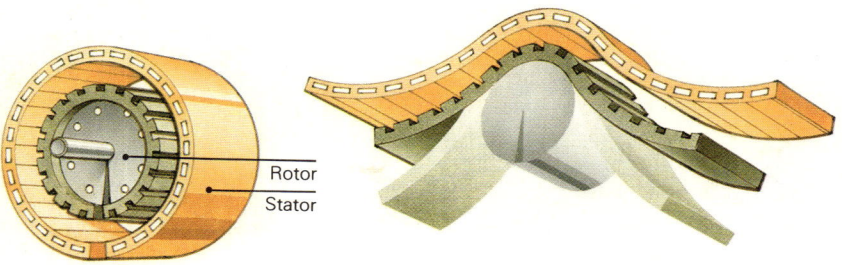
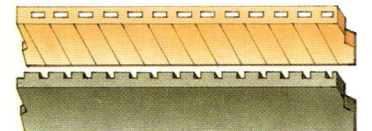

Left: A linear induction motor can be regarded as an opened-out conventional motor. In the conventional motor a rotor turns inside a fixed stator. If this is opened out and the flattened 'rotor' fixed, then the flattened 'stator' will move horizontally.

---

tender, was over 400 tonnes. On the level they could haul 3,000 tonnes at 112 km/hour.

Valves, in the steam box of a steam locomotive, are used to pass steam into the cylinder, first to one side of the piston and then to the other. Slide valves work against a flat surface in which the ports (openings) to the cylinder are situated. In a piston valve system the ports are located in the side of a cylinder and are opened and closed by 2 circular piston valve heads. Slide valves and piston valves move back and forth at the same rate as the piston. They are driven by a complicated system of cranks, rods and links called the valve gear, the position of which can be altered to cause the locomotive to reverse. Several types of valve gear have been devised, the most popular being Egide Walschaert's, invented in 1848. Some locomotives have camshaft-driven poppet valves similar to those of an internal combustion engine.

Victoria Falls Bridge across the Zambezi River is a steel arch bridge with a main span of 152 metres. It was built in 1905 to carry Cecil Rhodes's projected Cape-to-Cairo railway at a height of 400 metres above the river, spanning the spectacular gorge.

Watt, James (1736–1819) was a Scottish engineer. He not only improved NEWCOMEN'S engine but also made his own engines do more than merely act as pumps; almost any mechanical device could be powered by a Watt engine. In addition, he invented a governor — a device that controls the speed of an engine by reducing or increasing the steam supply to the cylinder as the engine goes faster or slower.

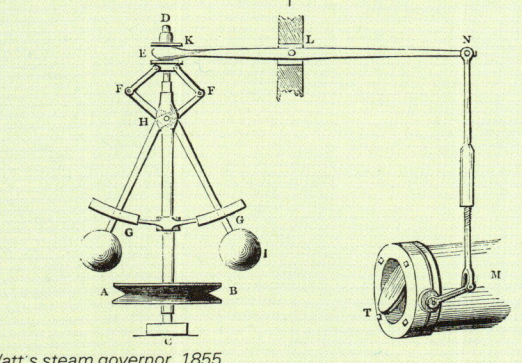

Watt's steam governor, 1855

The mastery of flight, one of man's earliest dreams, is another remarkable story of technological progress. It has culminated in the supersonic airliner and rockets, which are now probing the secrets of space.

Travelling through Air

Left: According to Greek legend Icarus, not heeding his father Daedalus's warning, flew too near the Sun. His wax wings melted and the goose feathers dropped out. Icarus plummeted into the sea and Daedalus returned home alone.

There are probably few people in the world who have not dreamed of being able to copy the birds and fly. Sadly, however, man is not built for flying unaided and we have had to develop machines to get into the air. But despite our technical achievements and superb modern aircraft, we have not nor will we ever manage to match the flight control of the birds.

Early attempts and ideas

It is fortunate that man in his attempts to fly has never been discouraged by failure. Many would-be aeronauts have plunged to their deaths, as the legendary Greek Icarus is supposed to have done 4,000 years ago when his wax wings melted in the heat of the Sun. Some were luckier. In about AD 1000 a Benedictine monk is said to have launched himself from a tower. The wings attached to his arms carried him 100 metres to a crash-landing in which he broke both legs. In later years many people tried strapping on wings and launching themselves off cliffs or towers. Generally, the result was a vertical fall, and a painful, often fatal, landing.

The reason for these disasters was a failure to understand how birds fly. People believed that birds flew by flapping their wings downwards and backwards and that they got off the ground because they were inherently light. This idea, based on the theories of the Greek philosopher Aristotle (384–322 BC), persisted until the 1800s. Meanwhile ideas for flying machines had been put forward. In the 1200s Friar Roger Bacon predicted the possibility of making 'Engines for flying' with 'artificiall Wings made to beat the Aire'. During the 1400s the Italian artist and scientist Leonardo da Vinci worked on this idea and designed a number of flying machines. However, he quickly realized that muscle-power was not enough to raise such machines off the ground and began designing soaring machines. Although these were based on mistaken ideas about how birds soared, in time Leonardo might have designed a practical glider.

Into the air

While some people were failing to copy the birds others managed to get into the air in a quite different way – by making machines lighter than air. In 1709 Bartolomeu de GUSMÃO demonstrated the first hot-air balloon in Portugal. This model balloon was made of thick paper and the hot air came from a small fire burning in an earthenware bowl. The Montgolfier brothers were unaware of this experiment when they too worked out that a container of hot air would rise. They demonstrated their first successful balloon

Reference

A Ader, Clement (1841–1925) built the *Eole* (wingspan 14 metres) in which he made the first uncontrolled 'hop' on October 9 1890. In 1897 his second aircraft *Avion* III failed to leave the ground.
Air speed indicator is an instrument that measures the difference in pressure between air rushing past the wing and still air. The forward movement of the aircraft causes an increase in pressure in a small open-ended, forward-pointing tube on the wing-tip.
Altimeter is an instrument that measures the decrease or increase in air pressure as an aircraft climbs or descends. It works in the same way as an aneroid barometer but measures the height above sea level.
Avro F (Britain, 1912) was the first aircraft with an enclosed cockpit. *Engine:* Viale 5-cylinder radial, 40 hp. *Wingspan:* 8.53 metres. *Speed:* 105 km/hour.
Avro Lancaster Mk. 1 (Britain, 1942) was the most famous bomber of World War II. 7,377 Lancasters were built and they carried out 156,000 missions. *Engines:* 4 Rolls-Royce Merlin X 12-cylinder V, 1,460 hp. *Wingspan:* 13.72 metres. *Max. speed:* 462 km/hour at 3,500 metres. *Crew:* 7. *Armament:* 10 machine guns, 9,980 kg of bombs.

Avro F

B Benoist XIV, a biplane seaplane, inaugurated the world's first scheduled passenger service between St Petersberg and Tampa, Florida, USA (34.5 km) in 1914. *Engine:* Roberts 6-cylinder in-line, 75 hp. *Wingspan:* 13.72 metres. *Max. speed:* 103 km/hour. *Crew:* 1. *Passenger:* 1.
Boeing 80A (America, 1928) was the second of the long line of successful Boeing civil transport aircraft (the first was the smaller 40A). The 80As remained in service until the arrival of the 247. *Engines:* 3 Pratt and Whitney Hornet 9-cylinder radial, 525 hp each. *Wingspan:* 24.38 metres. *Cruising speed:* 201 km/hour. *Crew:* 2-3. *Passengers:* 18.
Boeing 247 (America, 1933) made all other transport aircraft of the time obsolete. *Engines:* 2 Pratt and Whitney Wasp 9-cylinder radial, 550 hp each. *Wingspan:* 22.56 metres. *Cruising speed:* 250 km/hour. *Crew:* 2-3. *Passengers:* 10.
Boeing B-17G Flying Fortress (America, 1942) was the legendary bomber used in World War II for daylight

Above: A drawing of the third Montgolfier balloon flight on September 19 1783, in the presence of Louis XVI, Marie Antoinette and the French court. A basket was attached to the balloon and in it were placed a cock, a duck and a sheep. The balloon climbed to about 550 metres and landed just over 3 km away. The cock appeared somewhat the worse for wear, but investigation showed that he had not suffered from the high altitude; his appearance was probably the result of having been trampled by the sheep.

in France on April 25 1783 and the first manned flight in an untethered balloon was made on November 21 of the same year. Hot-air balloons were for many years replaced by gas balloons, but today hot-air ballooning has become a popular sport. Modern hot-air balloons take their fire with them, in the form of a flame fuelled by bottled gas. Thus their range is much greater than the Montgolfier balloons.

Gas balloons, filled with hydrogen or coal gas, were also invented in 1783, by Professor Jacques CHARLES. After 1852 engines and propellers were added and the first airships appeared, powered by steam or electricity. The arrival of the petrol engine in 1888 led to a rapid development of airships in the late 1800s and early 1900s, including the great German ZEPPELINS. These were dirigible (steerable) airships with the gas, usually hydrogen, contained in rigid aluminium envelopes. Many such airships were built in Germany, Britain and America. They were used by the armed forces during World War I and for carrying passengers. However, hydrogen is a dangerous, flammable gas. The inert gas helium was being used in some airships, but it was very expensive and often difficult to obtain. So, after several accidents with hydrogen-filled airships, notably the HINDENBURG and R.101 (see R.100) disasters, airship development came to an end. Today, only a few non-rigid airships are used for publicity purposes.

The first aeroplanes

Sir George CAYLEY was the first to work out how to produce lift without having flapping wings. In 1804 he built and flew a model glider – the first fixed-wing aircraft. In 1849 he built a triplane glider that carried a boy for several metres, and in 1859 he launched his coachman off in another triplane. The coachman promptly resigned, unaware that as the first man to fly in an aeroplane he had made history.

Cayley and others did considerable work on aerofoils and Otto Lilienthal used the knowledge so far gained to build a number of gliders between 1891 and 1896. Lilienthal had an understanding of bird flight and his aim was to build a workable ornithopter (a flapping-wing aircraft). To learn more about stability and control he built 18 different types of glider, all with bird-like, arched wings. Although he worked a great deal on control ideas, he never quite achieved full control of his gliders. In 1896, after failing to recover from a stall, he crashed, injuring himself fatally.

By this time there were a number of people searching for a method of powered flight. Many ideas were put forward and although some of these were, to us, outrageously funny, others were more practical. Clement ADER'S bat-like *Eole* was propelled by a steam engine. In 1890 this aircraft managed to hop 50 metres and was the first powered aircraft to take off. But it could not achieve sustained flight. The main problem with this and other experimental aircraft was lack of control. Aircraft builders were concentrating on stability and did not appear to see the need for control surfaces.

The final breakthrough came from the work of glider designers. Octave CHANUTE built a biplane hang-glider in which the wings were strongly braced. Although he too gave priority to the idea of stability, he gave great encouragement and assistance to two other glider enthusiasts, Wilbur and Orville Wright. Influenced by Chanute's design, these two brothers set about systematically designing aircraft in America.

In 1899 they built a glider that had a front elevator to control pitching and a fixed tailplane. The most important feature was the system of

---

raids over Europe. *Engines:* 4 Wright R-1820-97 Cyclone 9-cylinder radial, 1,200 hp. *Wingspan:* 31.62 metres. *Crew:* 10. *Armament:* 13 machine guns, 7.985 kg of bombs.
Boeing B-29 Superfortress (America, 1944) was the best strategic bomber of World War II and B-29s were operational during the Korean war. They are best remembered for two missions in 1949, when the first atomic bombs were dropped over Hiroshima and Nagasaki. *Engines:* 4 Wright R-3350-57 Cyclone 18-cylinder radial, 2,200 hp. *Wingspan:* 43.05 metres. *Max. speed:* 576 km/hour at 7,620 metres. *Crew:* 10. *Armament:* 20-mm cannon, 10 machine guns, 9,090 kg of bombs.
Boeing 707 (America, 1954) was the first jet airliner built by Boeing. *Engines:* 4 Pratt and Whitney JT3C turbojets, 5,625 kg thrust each. *Wingspan:* 39.9 metres. *Cruising speed:* 917 km/hour. *Passengers:* 179.
Boeing 747 (America, 1969) was the world's first wide-bodied airliner. *Engines:* 4 Pratt and Whitney JT9D turbojets, 22,680 kg thrust each. *Wingspan:* 59.64 metres. *Cruising speed:* 937 km/hour. *Passengers:* 385.
Bristol Beaufighter Mk. X (Britain, 1943) was used for anti-submarine warfare and ground attack for the last years of World War II. *Engines:* 2 Bristol Hercules XVII, 14-cylinder radial, 1,770 hp each. *Wingspan:* 17.63 metres. *Max. speed:* 531 km/hour at 400 metres. *Crew:* 2. *Armament:* 4 20-mm cannon, 964 kg torpedo, 226 kg of bombs.
Bubble sextant, unlike the marine SEXTANT (see page 79) does not need to be lined up with the horizon. Instead, a small bubble acts as an 'artificial horizon' and the index mirror is adjusted so that the Sun or star appears to sit in the centre of the bubble.

C Cayley, Sir George (1773–1857) was a British inventor. He built a successful glider and is now regarded as the 'father of aviation'.
Chanute, Octave (1832–

Boeing 707

Travelling through Air 51

Above: Otto Lilienthal with one of his gliders. He built six biplane and 12 monoplane gliders and controlled them in flight by altering the positions of his body.

Right: A modern hang glider banking to the right. The pilot uses the same method of control as Lilienthal.

Below: On December 14 1903 Wilbur Wright (1867–1912) first tried the Wright Flyer I. He crashed soon after take-off, slightly damaging the front elevator. On December 17 Orville Wright (1871–1948) made the first controlled powered flight. *Engine:* Wright 4-cylinder in-line, 12 hp. *Wingspan:* 12.29 metres. *Speed:* 48 km/hour.

wing warping (twisting) that enabled the glider to bank. Moving the control lever to the left caused cables to pull the trailing edge of the right wing-tip down and the trailing edge of the left wing-tip up. The result of this was that the aircraft banked to the left. However, they discovered that twisting the wing-tip downwards caused extra drag, resulting in a tendency for the glider to turn away from the bank. To counteract this effect they eventually added a rudder to the tail-plane.

By now the Wright brothers had more experience in flight than anyone before, and they built the Wright Flyer I, with a four-cylinder engine designed by themselves. At about 10.30 a.m. on December 17 1903, after an unsuccessful attempt three days before, Orville Wright flew a distance of 36.5 metres. Four more flights were made that day and on the last Wilbur flew a distance of 260 metres. The Wright brothers built three more aircraft and in 1905 made a flight of 39 kilometres. In 1908 Wilbur took a Wright Flyer IV to Europe.

Powered flight in Europe

During the years 1901–7 only a few Europeans were making much progress. Ferdinand Ferber was flying copies of Wright gliders and Gabriel VOISIN was experimenting with box-kite gliders.

1910) was an American railway engineer who became a glider designer and began building gliders in 1896.

Charles, Professor Jacques (1746–1823) designed and built the first hydrogen-filled balloon. It made its first ascent on August 27 1783 and on December 1, he and Marie-Noel Robert made the first ascent in a gas-filled balloon.

Consolidated B-24 Liberator (America, 1942) was the most widely used aircraft of World War II. Its main role was as a bomber and Liberators dropped about 635,000 tonnes of bombs and downed 4,189 enemy aircraft. *Engines:* 4 Pratt and Whitney R-1830-43 Twin Wasp 14-cylinder radial, 1,200 hp each. *Wingspan:* 33.52 metres. *Max. speed:* 488 km/hour at 7,620 metres. *Crew:* 8-10. *Armament:* 10 machine guns, 4,000 kg of bombs.

Curtiss, Glen (1878–1930) was an American pioneer aircraft builder. His aeroplanes won a number of competitions and he was noted particularly for his seaplanes. A Curtiss biplane made the first take-off from the deck of a ship. The Curtiss Aeroplane and Motor Company became famous for its naval aircraft.

Curtiss P-40B (America, 1941) was the most important American fighter in 1941-2 and was also used by the RAF, who designated it the Tomahawk Mk. II. *Engine:* Allison V-1710-33 12-cylinder V, 1,040 hp. *Wingspan:* 11.38 metres. *Max. speed:* 566 km/hour at 4,500 metres. *Crew:* 1. *Armament:* 4 machine guns (later ones carried bombs).

de Havilland, Sir Geoffrey (1882–1965) was a British aviation designer pioneer whose name is now linked with many aircraft.

de Havilland D.H.4A (Britain, 1919) was a modified version of the biplane D.H.4 bomber and was used to inaugurate the passenger service from London to Amsterdam. *Engine:* Rolls Royce Eagle VIII 12-cylinder V, 350 hp. *Wingspan:* 12.93 metres. *Max. speed:* 195 km/hour. *Crew:* 1. *Passengers:* 2.

Curtiss P-40B, 1941

Above: A replica of the Bleriot XI designed by Louis Bleriot (1872–1936). It used wing-warping for control and the first flight was made at Issy in France on January 23 1909. Raymond Saulnier later added several modifications that considerably improved the aircraft's performance. In the early morning of July 25 1909 Bleriot made the first cross-Channel flight from Calais to Dover in 36 minutes. *Engine:* Anzani 3-cylinder semi-radial, 22-25 hp. *Wingspan:* 7.8 metres. *Speed:* 58 km/hour.

However, the first powered flight in Europe was made by the Brazilian Alberto SANTOS-DUMONT, who had previously pioneered the development of the airship. On November 12 1906 he made six flights in his 14-*bis*, the last of which covered 220 metres. His aircraft was a curious affair with the tailplane at the front and the propeller at the rear, and it was the first aeroplane to use ailerons. However, this idea did not catch on and Santos-Dumont went on to design the Demoiselles, small monoplanes with wing-warping for control.

By 1907 Gabriel Voisin and Henri FARMAN were achieving success with box-kite aeroplanes. Louis Blériot, who had been Voisin's assistant, was building monoplanes that resembled modern aeroplanes, with tails at the rear and puller propellers. However, they were all still a long way behind the Wright brothers. In 1908 Wilbur amazed everyone with two-hour flights in his Wright Flyer IV. This, at last, convinced the Europeans that control was necessary and in 1908 Farman added ailerons to a Voisin-Farman aircraft and flew a distance of 27 kilometres. On July 25 1909 Blériot flew his XI across the English Channel to accomplish the first-ever crossing.

How aeroplanes fly

The wings of an aeroplane are described as aerofoils because they produce lift and it is these aerofoils that cause the craft to fly. In cross-section an aerofoil can be seen to have a particular shape. Air travelling over the upper, curved surface has farther to go than air travelling over the flatter, lower surface. As a result, the air travelling over the upper surface moves faster, its pressure is reduced and the consequent higher pressure on the lower surface of the wing produces lift.

The angle at which the wing meets the air (angle of attack) is important. Increasing the angle increases the lift up to a certain point. If the angle is increased beyond this point, the air

---

de Havilland D.H.82A Tiger Moth (Britain, 1931) was developed from the 1925 D.H.60 Moth. A total of 7,300 Tiger Moths were built and were used by the RAF for 15 years. Many ended up in civil aviation and there are still a number of airworthy planes. *Engine:* de Havilland Gypsy Major 4-cylinder in-line, 130 hp. *Wingspan:* 8.94 metres. *Max. speed:* 167 km/hour. *Crew:* 2.

Tiger Moths

de Havilland Mosquito Mk. I (Britain, 1941) was built as a fast reconnaissance aircraft. Because of its success, later versions were built as fighter bombers, the best of which was the Mk. VI. *Engines:* 2 Rolls Royce Merlin XXI 12-cylinder V, 1,460 hp each. *Wingspan:* 16.51 metres. *Max. speed:* 611 km/hour. *Crew:* 2. *Armament:* 4 20-mm cannon, 4 machine guns, 907 kg of bombs.

de Havilland Comet I (Britain, 1952) was the world's first turbojet airliner. *Engines:* 4 de Havilland Ghost turbojets, 2,018 kg thrust each. *Wingspan:* 35.05 metres. *Cruising speed:* 789 km/hour. *Passengers:* 36. A later version, the Comet 4, made the first transatlantic jet crossing in 1958.

Dornier Do 217 (Germany, 1940) was the successor to the 1939 Do 17 bomber and various versions were used as reconnaissance aircraft, torpedo-carriers and night fighters. The Do 217E-1 was a bomber. *Engines:* 2 BMW 801 MA 14-cylinder radial, 1,580 hp each. *Wingspan:* 19.00 metres. *Max. speed:* 515 km/hour at 5,200 metres. *Crew:* 4. *Armament:* 5 machine guns, 15-mm cannon, 2,000 kg of bombs.

Douglas DC-2 (America, 1934) was the first of a long line of successful low-wing monoplanes, leading to the modern jets, the DC-8 and the wide-bodied DC-10. *Engines:* 2 Wright Cyclone F.3 9-cylinder radial, 710 hp each. *Wingspan:* 25.91 metres. *Cruising speed:* 273 km/hour. *Crew:* 2-3. *Passengers:* 4.

Drag is caused when some of the energy of a forward-moving aircraft is absorbed, and it is produced in 3 ways. First, energy is absorbed by the action of pushing the air aside as the aircraft moves forward; streamlining helps to reduce this. Second, the inner layer of air tends to stick to the surface of the aircraft, forming a boundary layer of slow-moving air, and energy is absorbed by friction. Third, energy is ab-

Travelling through Air 53

moving over the upper surface becomes turbulent, causing a loss of lift, and the aircraft stalls.

Three other forces act on a wing. In constant, level flight the lift is balanced by the weight of the aircraft, as gravity tries to pull it towards the ground. As well as producing lift the forward movement of the wing through the air produces DRAG, which resists the forward motion. This is balanced by the thrust produced by the aircraft engines.

The control surfaces are operated by cables attached to the control column in the cockpit. The ailerons on each wing are used in keeping the aircraft level and in turning. For example, lowering the port (left) aileron raises the port wing by increasing its curvature and causing it to generate more lift. The aircraft thus banks (tilts) to the right. If, at the same time, the rudder is pushed to starboard (right) the aircraft turns in that direction. On the tail-plane the elevators act in the same way as the ailerons, but they are both used together in order to make the aircraft dive or climb.

Since 1935 several more control surfaces have been added, particularly to high-speed aircraft. Flaps on the trailing edges of wings are used to generate more lift during take-off and to increase drag during landing. Leading edge flaps reduce

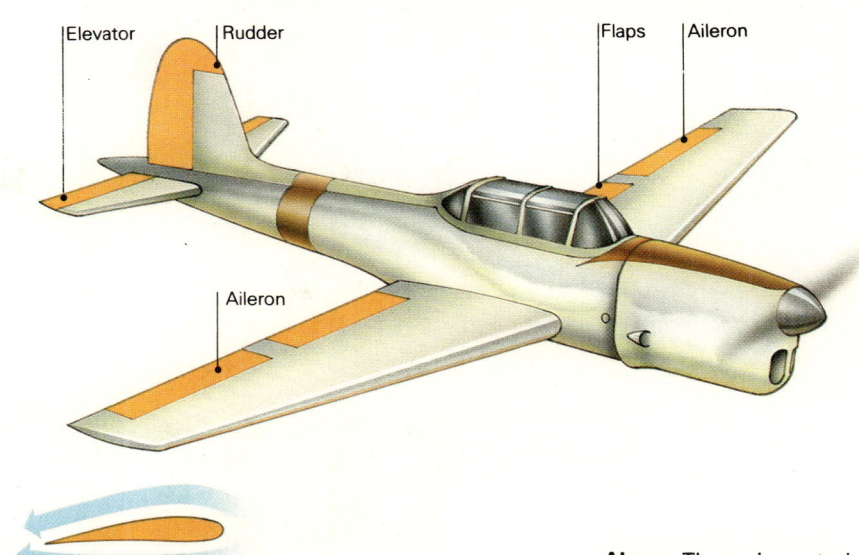

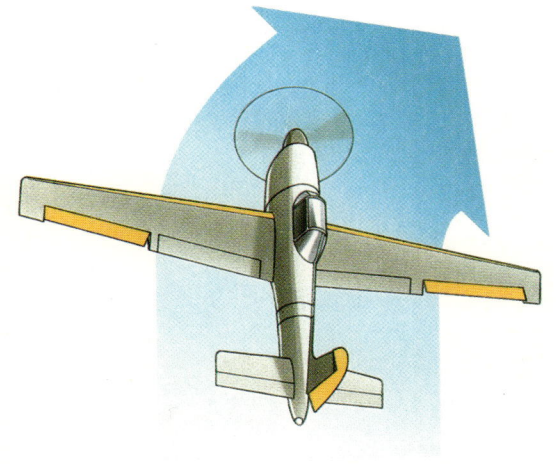

Above: A cross-section of an aerofoil.

Right: Yawing, a side-to-side movement of the aircraft, is prevented by the sides of the fuselage and the tail fin. Pitching, an up-and-down movement of the aircraft, is prevented by the horizontal surface of the tailplane.

Right: In a balanced turn the wings have to provide extra lift to produce the centripetal force that holds the aircraft in the turn as well as balancing its weight. The combination of the centrifugal force (the reaction to the centripetal force) and the weight of the aircraft produces a force sometimes known as the 'G force' which balances the overall lift.

Right: The elevators on the tailplane are used to make the aircraft climb or dive. If the control column is pulled back, the elevators are deflected upwards. The lift on the tailplane therefore decreases and the nose rises. When the control column is pushed forward, the elevators are deflected downwards. The lift on the tailplane therefore increases and the nose drops.

Above: The main control surfaces of an aircraft.

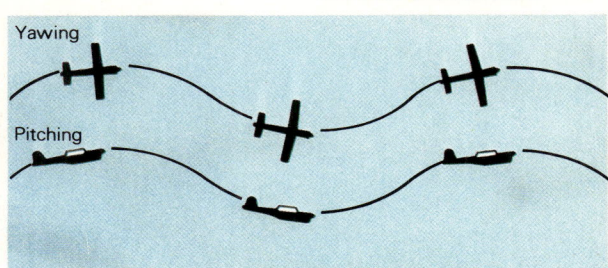

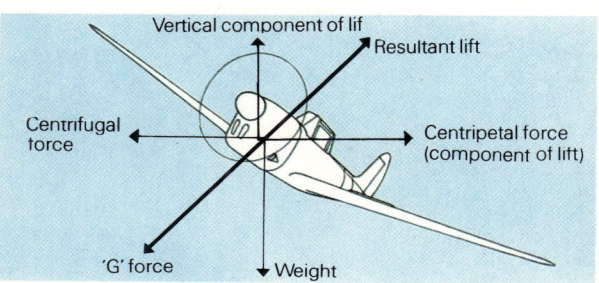

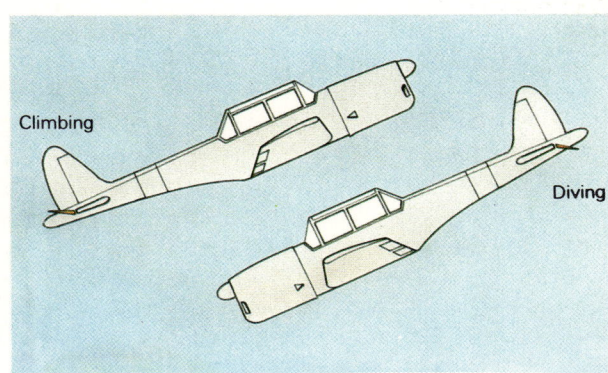

Above: To turn the aircraft the pilot uses the rudder and the ailerons. In turning to starboard (right) the rudder is deflected to the right. At the same time the aircraft is banked to the right by lowering the port (left) aileron (causing an increase in lift on the port wing) and raising the starboard aileron.

---

sorbed by the vortices (spirals) of air created at the wing-tips.

Farman, Henri (1874–1958) was a British-born aircraft builder. He built his first aircraft in France in 1909 and became a naturalized French citizen in 1937.
Farman F.60 Goliath (France, 1919) was a highly successful civil transport aircraft that broke several world records. *Engines:* 2 Salmson CM 9-cylinder radial, 260 hp each. *Wingspan:* 26.46 metres. *Cruising speed:* 120 km/hour at 2,000 metres. *Crew:* 2. *Passengers:* 12.
Focke-Wulf Fw2 190A-1 (Germany, 1941) was an even better fighter than the Messerschmitt Bf 109. A later version was a fighter bomber. *Engine:* BMW 801C-1 14-cylinder radial, 1,600 hp. *Wingspan:* 10.50 metres. *Max. speed:* 626 km/hour at 5,500 metres. *Crew:* 1. *Armament:* 4 machine guns, 2 20-mm cannon.
Fokker, Anthony (1890–1939) was the great Dutch aircraft designer who founded companies in Germany and Holland and became famous for his World War I aircraft.
Fokker E III (Germany, 1915), a monoplane fighter, was named the 'Scourge' because at the time it was the only aircraft with a synchronized, forward-firing machine gun. *Engine:* Oberusel U1 9-cylinder rotary, 100 hp. *Wingspan:* 9.41 metres. *Max. speed:* 140 km/hour. *Crew:* 2. *Armament:* 1-2 machine guns.
Fokker Dr I (Germany, 1917) was a triplane fighter with outstanding manoeuvrability. *Engine:* Thulin-built Le Rhône 9J 9-cylinder rotary, 110 hp. *Wingspan:* 7.19 metres. *Max. speed:* 165 km/hour at 4,000 metres. *Crew:* 1. *Armament:* 2 machine guns.
Fokker D VII (Germany, 1918), a biplane, was the finest fighter of World War I. *Engine:* Mercedes D ILI 6-cylinder in-line, 160 hp.

Fokker D VII

Wingspan: 8.9 metres. *Max. speed:* 200 km/hour. *Crew:* 1. *Armament:* 2 machine guns.

Gloster Meteor (Britain, 1943) was the first British jet fighter. Meteors never saw action against the Messerschmitt 262, but the Mk. I version was used to shoot down V-1 flying bombs. The Mk. III took part in a few missions over Germany in 1945. *Engines:* 2 Rolls Royce Derwent 1,907 kg thrust. *Wingspan:* 13.11 metres. *Max. speed:* 667 km/hour at 3,000 metres.

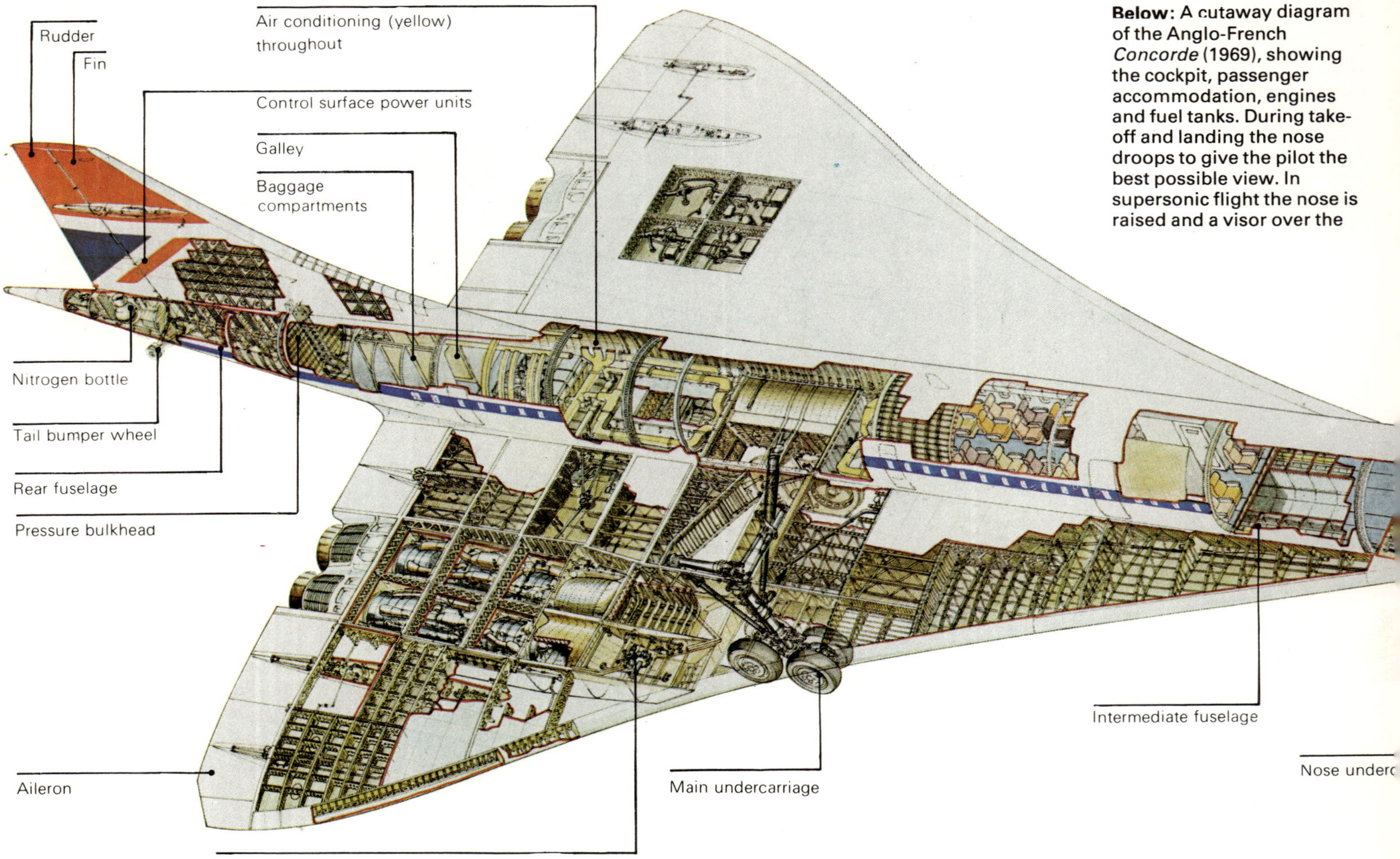

Travelling through Air

Below: A cutaway diagram of the Anglo-French *Concorde* (1969), showing the cockpit, passenger accommodation, engines and fuel tanks. During take-off and landing the nose droops to give the pilot the best possible view. In supersonic flight the nose is raised and a visor over the

air turbulence allowing aircraft to achieve higher angles of attack without stalling. Spoilers are vertical flaps near the trailing edge of a wing used to assist in banking and to increase drag during landing.

Aircraft development

From 1909 to 1914 aircraft were used mostly for sport and trials. Racing competitions, such as the Gordon Bennett Aviation Cup (1909) and the Schneider Trophy (1913), were organized and speed records were constantly being broken. The first manufacturing company had been set up in France by Gabriel and Charles Voisin. In America Glen CURTISS was building seaplanes and in Europe Geoffrey DE HAVILLAND and Anthony FOKKER, two men who were to become

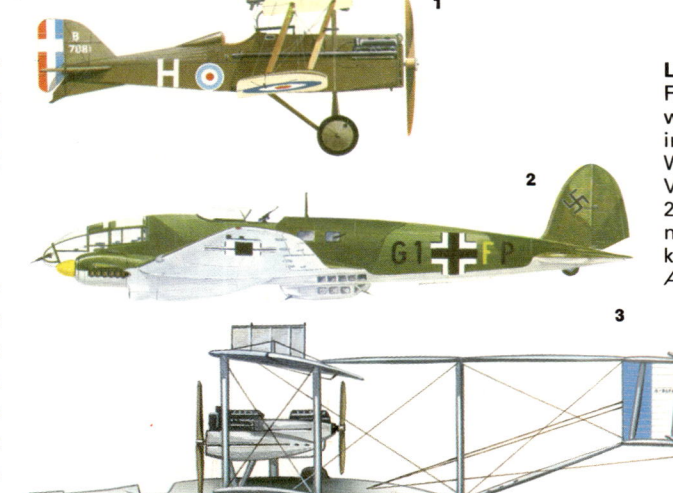

Left: 1. The Royal Aircraft Factory S.E.5a (Britain, 1917) was one of the best fighters in the last year of World War I. *Engine:* Wolseley W.4 Viper 8-cylinder in-line V, 200 hp. *Wingspan:* 8.12 metres. *Max. speed:* 222 km/hour. *Crew:* 1. *Armament:* 2 machine guns.

Crew: 1. *Armament:* 4 20-mm cannon.

Graf Zeppelin (Germany, 1928) was a luxurious intercontinental passenger airship. Designated LZ 227, the Graf Zeppelin completed 590 flights, including 140 across the Atlantic. By 1940, when the airship was scrapped, it had flown 1,695,252 km. *Engines:* 5 Machbach, 550 hp each. *Length:* 236.60 metres. *Diameter:* 30.5 metres. *Cruising speed:* 109 km/hour. *Crew:* 45. *Passengers:* 20.

Gusmão, Bartolomeu de (1686–1727) was a Brazilian priest. On August 8 1709, in Portugal, he demonstrated the first hot-air balloon, which rose 3.6 metres off the ground.

Handley Page 0/400 (Britain, 1916) was a heavy bomber used for both

Handley Page HP42

day and night raids in World War I. *Engines:* 2 Rolls Royce Eagle VIII 12-cylinder in-line V, 360 hp each. *Wingspan:* 30.48 metres. *Max. speed:* 157 km/hour. *Crew:* 4. *Armament:* 4-5 machine guns, 907 kg of bombs.

Handley Page HP42E (Britain, 1931) was a large biplane passenger transport used by Imperial Airways until 1939, even after it had been superseded by newer aircraft. *Engines:* 4 Bristol Jupiter XIF, 9-cylinder radial, 550 hp each. *Wingspan:* 39.62 metres. *Cruising speed:* 160 km/hour. *Crew:* 2. *Passengers:* 24.

Handley Page Halifax (Britain, 1944) was one of the finest bombers of World War I. It was also used for dropping paratroops and towing gliders. One of the best versions was the Mk. II. *Engines:* 4 Bristol Hercules XVI 14-cylinder radial, 1,615 hp. *Wingspan:* 31.75 metres. *Max. speed:* 454 km/hour at 4,100 metres. *Crew:* 7. *Armament:* 9 machine guns, 5,890 kg of bombs.

Hawker Hurricane Mk. I (Britain, 1937) was the RAF's first monoplane fighter. During 1940 Hurricanes accounted for more than half the German aircraft shot down. Later versions were built as night fighters and fighter bombers. *Engine:* Rolls Royce Merlin II 12-cylinder V, 1,030 hp. *Wingspan:* 12.19 metres. *Max.*

Travelling through Air

cockpit window helps in streamlining. *Engines:* 4 Rolls Royce/SNECMA Olympus 593 Mk 602 turbojets, 17,259 kg thrust each. *Wingspan:* 25.55 metres. *Max. cruising speed:* 2,179 km/hour. *Crew:* 3. *Passengers:* 128–144.

Right: A Douglas DC-3 (America, 1936) still in use. The DC-3 was the successor to the DC-2 and during World War II it became the most versatile of all transport aircraft. *Engines:* 2 Pratt and Whitney 9-cylinder radial, 1,200 hp each. *Wingspan:* 28.96 metres. *Cruising speed:* 290 km/hour. *Crew:* 2. *Passengers:* 14–32.

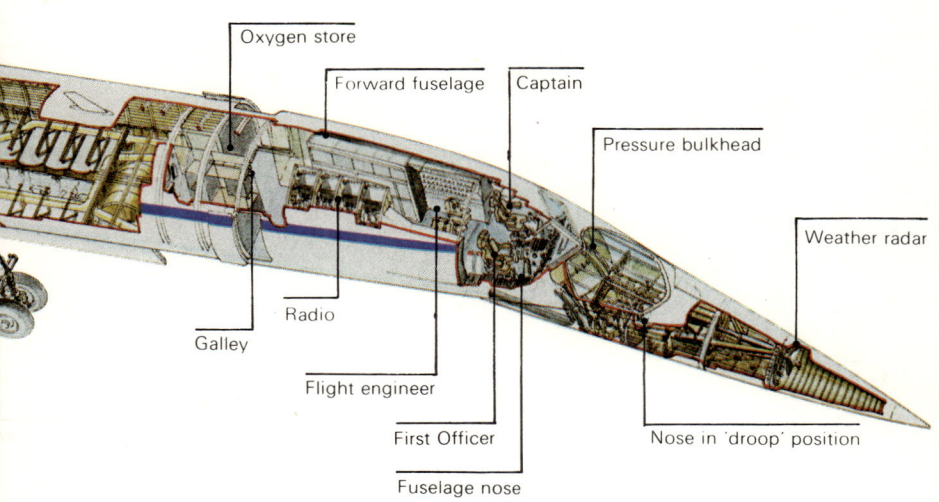

2. The Heinkel He IIIH-2 (Germany, 1939) was the Luftwaffe's main bomber at the beginning of World War II. *Engines:* 2 Junkers Jumo 211A-3 12-cylinder V, 1.100 hp each. *Wingspan:* 22.60 metres. *Max. speed:* 405 km/hour. *Crew:* 5. *Armament:* 6 machine guns, 2,495 kg of bombs.

3. A Navy/Curtiss NC-4 (America, 1919) was the first aeroplane to complete the Atlantic crossing in May 1919, from Trepassy Bay, Newfoundland, to Lisbon, Portugal, stopping at the Azores on the way. *Engines:* 4 Liberty 12 12-cylinder V, 400 hp each. *Wingspan:* 38.40 metres. *Max. speed:* 137 km/hour. *Crew:* 6.

famous, were also building aeroplanes. In 1912 the British designer Alliot Roe built the AVRO F, which was the first aeroplane to have an enclosed cockpit. In Russia Igor SIKORSKY built the first four-engined aeroplane, the *Russkii Vitiaz*, which flew in 1913.

At the beginning of World War I aircraft were seen as only being useful for reconnaissance and a number of aircraft were built for this purpose. However, war in the air soon escalated. The first aircraft equipped with machine guns were the French MORANE-SAULNIER Ls in 1915. In the same year the Germans introduced the 'Scourge' — the monoplane Fokker E III (Eindekker) — which had a forward-firing machine-gun synchronized to fire in between the blades of the propeller. By the end of World War I both sides had a number of fighters, including the Royal Aircraft Factory S.E.5a, the SOPWITH Camel, the FOKKER D VII and the Fokker Dr I (the aircraft flown by Manfred von Richthofen, the 'Red Baron'). For bombing the Germans used Zeppelin airships until 1917, when they were replaced with strategic bombers, such as the Zeppelin (Staaken) R VI. British bombers in use by 1918 included the HANDLEY PAGE 0/400 and the VICKERS Vimy.

The valuable experience gained during World War I was put to more constructive use during the years that followed. In 1919 John Alcock and Arthur Whitten Brown made their historic non-stop crossing of the Atlantic Ocean in a Vickers Vimy. By now engines were more powerful, and it had become possible to build aircraft to carry passengers. After the war, airline services opened in Germany, France and Britain and the first international service was established by a British company, Aircraft Transport and Travel, using war-surplus bombers, DE HAVILLAND D.H.4As.

The first all-metal aircraft, the Junkers J 1, had been built in 1915. After the war the Germans were forbidden by the terms of the Versailles treaty to build large aeroplanes and so they turned their attention to high-performance aircraft. They built the JUNKERS F 13, successor to the J 1, and this excellent four-passenger seaplane saw service with about 30 airlines around the world. Another important civil aeroplane of the time was the FARMAN F.60 Goliath.

By the early 1930s airlines were carrying passengers to many parts of the world, and aircraft with large passenger-carrying capacities had been built. Many experimental designs

speed: 515 km/hour at 6,100 metres. *Crew:* 1. *Armament:* 8 machine guns.
Heinkel He 178 (Germany, 1939) was the world's first jet aircraft. *Engine:* HeS 3B, 498 kg thrust. *Wingspan:* 7.09 metres. *Max. speed:* 708 km/hour.
Heinkel He 219A-2/R1 (Germany, 1943) was the Luftwaffe's finest night fighter. The first prototype shot down at least 25 British bombers in 10 days. The He 219 was also the first aircraft equipped with ejector seats. *Engines:* 2 Daimler Benz DB 603A 12-cylinder V, 1,750 hp each. *Wingspan:* 18.50 metres. *Max. speed:* 670 km/hour at 7,000 metres. *Crew:* 2. *Armament:* 6 20-mm cannon.
Hindenburg (Germany, 1936), designated LZ 129, was the world's largest airship. For about a year it operated a passenger service between Frankfurt and New York. On May 6 1937 it caught fire over Lakehurst, New Jersey, and 35 of the 97 people on board were killed. *Engines:* 4 Daimler Benz, 1,320 hp each. *Length:* 245 metres. *Diameter:* 41.20 metres. *Max. speed:* 135 km/hour. *Crew:* 40. *Passengers:* 50.

Junkers F 13 (Germany, 1919) was a highly-successful all-metal small transport aircraft. *Engine:* BMW 111A 6-cylinder in-line, 185 hp. *Wingspan:* 17.75 metres. *Cruising speed:* 140 km/hour. *Crew:* 2. *Passengers:* 4.
Junkers Ju 87D1 (Germany, 1938) was the well-known and much-feared 'Stuka' dive-bomber of World War II. *Engine:* Junkers Jumo 211 J-1 12-cylinder V, 1,400 hp. *Wingspan:* 13.79 metres. *Max. speed:* 410 km/hour at 4,100 metres. *Crew:* 2. *Armament:* 4 machine guns, 1,800 kg of bombs.
Junkers Ju 88 (Germany, 1939) was the Luftwaffe's most versatile aircraft. More than 16,000 were built and were used for reconnaissance, ground-attack, bombing, dive-bombing and torpedo bombing. The Ju 88G-7 was a formidable night fighter. *Engines:* 2 Junkers Jumo 213E 12-cylinder V, 1,725 hp each. *Wingspan:* 20.80

Hindenburg

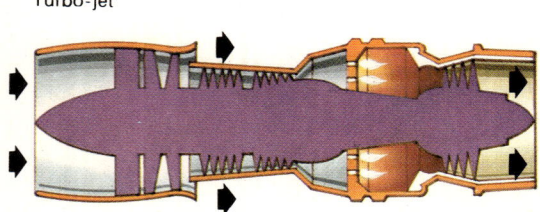
Turbo-jet

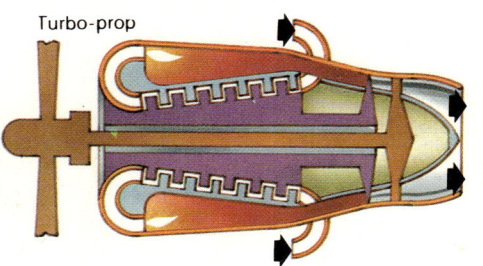
Turbo-prop

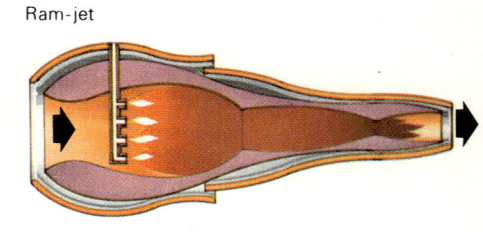
Ram-jet

appeared and some of these had short lives; others even failed to get off the ground. However, there were also many successes. By 1935 famous passenger transport included the enormous flying boats, such as Imperial Airways' SHORT S.8 Calcutta and Pan American's MARTIN M-130 China Clippers and Sikorsky S-42s. Land aircraft included the Handley Page H.P.42s, which were virtually synonymous with Imperial Airways for many years, and the Boeing 80A. These aircraft were superseded by the Boeing 247 and Douglas DC-2. These all-metal, low-wing monoplanes, with their new technology and advanced design and performance, marked the beginning of a new era.

Alongside the success of large commercial aircraft there had also been considerable development of smaller types, including fighters, trainers, civil transporters, racers and private aircraft. Among the most famous of these were the Ryan NYP SPIRIT OF ST LOUIS, in which Charles Lindbergh made the first solo, non-stop Atlantic crossing in 1927, the Fokker F VIIb-3m SOUTHERN CROSS, in which Charles Kingsford Smith made the first crossing of the Pacific in 1928, and the de Havilland D.H.82A Tiger Moth, which is probably the best-known training aircraft in the world.

By the beginning of World War II the biplane fighters of the early 1930s had been outdated by the new sleek monoplanes. In 1939 the German Luftwaffe had 1,200 fighters, including the formidable MESSERSCHMITT Bf 109 (popularly known as the Me 109), which could outclass all other fighters. In Britain the RAF had fewer aeroplanes, but despite this disadvantage the squadrons of the now-famous HAWKER Hurricanes and SUPERMARINE SPITFIRES won the Battle of Britain. Later well-known British World War II fighters included the multirole de Havilland Mosquito and the BRISTOL BEAUFIGHTER, which was equipped with an early version of radar for night interception. In Germany the Bf 109 was joined by the FOCKE-WULF Fw 190, possibly Germany's best fighter, and the HEINKEL He 219. New fighters appeared throughout the world and the best of these included the American Lockheed P-38 Lightnings, which destroyed more enemy aircraft in the Pacific than any other fighter, and the outstanding Japanese MITSUBISHI A6M2 Reisen, or Zero.

Strategic bombing played an important part in World War II. Among the bombers that carried out missions over Britain were the Heinkel He 111, the DORNIER Do 217, many of which were later converted into night fighters, and the multirole Junkers Ju 88, which was the German equivalent of the Mosquito. In Britain a number of bombers were developed, including the well-known VICKERS WELLINGTON and the later Avro Lancaster, which took part in some famous raids, such as the 'Dam Busters' mission in May 1943. American bombers included the Boeing B-17 Flying Fortress, which was also used for long-range reconnaissance, and the CONSOLIDATED B-24 Liberator, of which 18,000 were built, more than any other American aircraft.

The jet age

As in all forms of transport the development of aircraft has progressed with the development of engines. The invention of the internal combustion engine enabled the Wright brothers to fly the first successful powered aircraft. Progressively more advanced engines were developed over the years and the size, endurance and speed of aircraft increased accordingly.

However, the greatest leap forward came with the invention of the gas turbine jet engine, developed by Sir Frank WHITTLE between 1928 and 1939. The jet engine has a much greater

Above: Four types of jet engine. In a turbojet the compressor draws air into the engine and compresses it. Fuel is injected into the combustion chamber, where it ignites in the hot, compressed air. The expanding gases drive the turbine as they leave the rear of the engine. In a turboprop engine the compressor again compresses the air before fuel is injected into the combustion chambers. However, the turbine not only drives the compressor but also a propeller, which helps to power the aircraft. The pulse jet and ramjet have no compressors. Instead, the air is compressed by the forward movement of the engine itself. As a result they can only be used when the craft is already moving. The pulse jet, which was the type used on the German V-1 flying bombs in World War II, has valves that open and close by pressure in the combustion chamber, and combustion takes the form of a series of explosions. The ramjet produces a continuous stream of hot gases.

metres. *Max speed:* 626 km/hour at 9,000 metres. *Crew:* 4. *Armament:* 6 20-mm cannon, 1 machine gun.
Lockheed P-38 Lightning (America, 1942) was a powerful high-altitude interceptor fighter. The best version was the P-38J. *Engines:* 2 Allison V-1710-91 12-cylinder V, 1,425 hp each. *Wingspan:* 15.85 metres. *Max speed:* 666 km/hour at 7,600 metres. *Crew:* 1. *Armament:* 20-mm cannon, 14 machine guns, 1,450 kg of bombs.
Lockheed L-1011 Tristar

Lockheed L-1011 Tristar

(America, 1970) is a wide-bodied jet airliner. *Engines:* 3 Rolls Royce RB. 211 turbofan, 19,050 kg thrust. *Wingspan:* 47.34 metres. *Cruising speed:* 901 km/hour at 10,700 metres. *Passengers:* 400.

Mach number is the speed of an aircraft expressed as a multiple of the speed of sound; i.e. Mach 2 is twice the speed of sound. It is expressed in this way because the speed of sound varies with the temperature and pressure of the air and is lower at high altitudes than at sea level. The speed of sound at 0°C at sea level is 1,194 km/hour.
Martin M-130 China Clippers (America, 1930) were 3 flying boats flown overseas. *Engines:* 4 Pratt and Whitney Twin Wasp 14-cylinder radial, 830 hp each. *Wingspan:* 39.70 metres. *Cruising speed:* 266 km/hour. *Crew:* 5. *Passengers:* 48.
McDonnell-Douglas Phantom F-4 (America, 1958) is a modern jet fighter of which many versions have been built. *Engines:* 2

General Electric J-19-17 turbojets. *Wingspan:* 11.7 metres. *Max. speed:* 1,464 km/hour. *Crew:* 2. *Armament:* 4 AIM Sparrow missiles, 20-mm multibarrel cannon, 7,620 kg of bombs.
Messerschmitt Bf 109 (Germany, 1935) was for 5 years the best fighter in the world. More than 35,000 were built in several versions. The 1939 version, which fought in the Battle of Britain, was the Bf 109E-1. *Engine:* Daimler Benz DB 601A 12-cylinder V 1,050 hp. *Wingspan:* 9.87 metres. *Max. speed:* 550 km/hour at

Travelling through Air

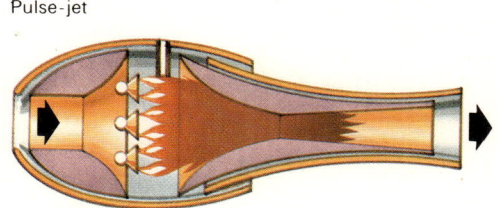
Pulse-jet

power than a piston engine and, when jet engines began to be introduced into aircraft during the last years of World War II, the scene was set for reaching hitherto undreamed of speeds.

The first jet aircraft to fly was the HEINKEL He 178 in 1939 and the first jet fighter used in action was the Messerschmitt 262. The GLOSTER METEOR, the direct result of Sir Frank Whittle's work, took to the air in 1943.

Today, most aircraft are powered by jet engines. New designs, such as arrow-shaped swept wings and delta wings, have been introduced to cope with increasing speeds. Jet fighters built since World War II include the American MCDONNELL-DOUGLAS Phantoms and the Russian Mikoyan MiGs. The first jet airliner was the de Havilland D.H.106 Comet I and this aircraft showed up a major problem of high-altitude flying. In 1953 and 1954 three Comet Is broke up in the air. Eventually metal fatigue of the pressure cabin was diagnosed as being the cause. In recent years the most successful jet airliners have been the Boeings, beginning with the Boeing 707s in 1958 and leading to the gigantic, wide-bodied Boeing 747 Jumbos in 1973, the largest of which can hold 500 passengers.

Above left: The Hawker Siddeley Harrier GR 3 (Britain, 1966) is a ground attack aircraft, capable of taking off vertically and of slow, low-level flight as well as high-speed flight. *Engine:* Bristol Siddeley Pegasus 103 vectored thrust turbofan, 1,752 kg thrust. *Wingspan:* 7.69 metres. *Max. speed:* 1,158 km/hour. *Crew:* 1. *Armament:* 2 30-mm guns and up to 2,270 kg of bombs, including 68-mm SNEB rockets or sidewinder missiles.

Above: A helicopter can be used almost anywhere. In this case one is being employed to transport skiers to the upper slopes of a snow-covered mountain.

The first jet aircraft that could fly faster than the speed of sound (*see* MACH NUMBER) in level flight was the NORTH AMERICAN F-100 Super Sabre in 1953. Today there are many supersonic aircraft, including the latest jet airliners, the Russian TUPOLEV Tu 144 and the Anglo-French Concorde. Supersonic flight has also involved changes in design. The shock wave generated by an aircraft travelling near, at or faster than the speed of sound causes additional drag. To overcome this designers have used thin, highly swept back wings and symmetrical aerofoil sections with pointed leading and trailing edges. Some supersonic aircraft, such as the American ROCKWELL B-1 bomber, have variable geometry, or swing wings. At high speeds the wings are swung back to reduce the amount of lift and the effects of the shock waves.

Vertical take-off and landing

The idea of taking off vertically is nearly as old as the idea of flight. Leonardo da Vinci designed helicopters, George Cayley built models, and a number of other inventors designed machines, most of which were totally impractical. The first helicopter capable of carrying a man was

---

4,000 metres. *Crew:* 1. *Armament:* 2 machine guns, 2 20-mm cannon.
Messerschmitt 262A-1a (Germany, 1944) was the first jet fighter to see action.

Messerschmitt Bf 109

Faster than any other fighter of its time it might have changed the course of World War II if it had been used as a daytime fighter. Instead it was used for reconnaissance and as a bomber and night fighter. *Engines:* 2 Junkers Jumo 004B-1, 898 kg thrust. *Wingspan:* 12.48 metres. *Max. speed:* 869 km/hour at 6,000 metres. *Crew:* 1. *Armament:* 4 30-mm cannon.
Mitsubishi A6M2 Reisen (Japan, 1940) was used in the attack on Pearl Harbor (1941) and later versions were used in suicide missions in 1945. *Engine:* Nakajima NK1C Sakee 12 14-cylinder radial, 950 hp. *Wingspan:* 12.10 metres. *Max. speed:* 534 km/hour at 4,500 metres. *Crew:* 1. *Armament:* 2 20-mm cannon, 2 machine guns, 120 kg of bombs.
Morane-Saulnier L (France, 1913) was a monoplane fighter. In 1915 it was fitted with a machine gun that fired through the propeller area. The blades had steel plates to deflect bullets. *Engine:* Gnome rotary, 80 hp. *Wingspan:* 11.2 metres. *Max. speed:* 115 km/hour at 2,000 metres. *Crew:* 1-2. *Armament:* 1-2 machine guns, a few bombs.

Nakajima Ki-84-1a Hayate (Japan, 1943) was one of the finest Japanese fighters of World War II. *Engine:* Nakajima Ha-45 18-cylinder radial, 1,900 hp. *Wingspan:* 11.23 metres. *Max. speed:* 631 km/hour at 6,100 metres. *Crew:* 1. *Armament:* 2 20-mm cannon, 500 kg of bombs.
North American P-51D Mustang (America, 1944) was one of America's best World War II fighters. A total of 7,966 were built. *Engine:* Packard V-1650-7 12-cylinder V, 1,510 hp. *Wingspan:* 11.28 metres. *Max. speed:* 703 km/hour at 7,600 metres. *Crew:* 1. *Armament:* 6 machine guns, 907 kg of bombs.

designed by the Frenchman Paul Cornu in 1907. However, it had engineering and stability problems that could not be overcome at the time. In 1942 in America Igor Sikorsky built the first practical helicopter, the VS-316A (which was designated R-4 by the military).

The blades of a helicopter have an aerofoil cross-section to provide lift. The pitch of the blades (the angle at which they meet the air) can be altered to generate more lift in climbing or less lift when descending. The reaction of a helicopter to the torque (twisting force) produced by a horizontally-spinning rotor is a tendency to spin uncontrollably in the opposite direction. The various configurations of helicopters are designed to overcome this by balancing the torque using a vertical rotor at the rear, a second horizontal rotor spinning in the opposite direction or a single horizontal rotor propelled by jets at the tips of the blades.

Today there are many uses for helicopters, generally in situations where it is impossible or inconvenient to use conventional aircraft. They are used in air-sea rescue, aerial-crane work, off-shore drilling operations, passenger transport across cities, and warfare.

Research into Vertical Take-Off and Landing (VTOL) aircraft began seriously in the 1950s, when Rolls Royce tried out two jet engines on a test machine made of tubular steel, called the Flying Bedstead. The success of this experimental craft led to the first VTOL aircraft, the Short Brothers and Harland SC-1, which had separate lift and propulsion jets. Over the years various systems have been tried, including jets that can be tilted and propellers mounted on tilt-wings. By far the most successful is the system of vectored (directed) thrust first devised in 1960. In this system the jet engines are fixed and the hot gases are directed either downwards or backwards through swivelling nozzles. The first fully-operational VTOL aircraft was the Hawker Siddeley Harrier, which entered service in 1968 and is the world's most versatile aircraft.

Aircraft navigation

In the early days of flying there were no sophisticated navigational aids. A pilot would often find his position by flying low and reading the name of a railway station (later, some stations had their names written in large white letters on the roof). One way of navigating was to fly from one landmark to the next and to follow railway lines.

It was soon discovered that the wind affected the flight path of an aircraft, causing it to drift off course. Thus, a navigational system known as dead reckoning had to be used. In this system a pilot, knowing the wind speed and direction, works out the necessary compass heading of the aircraft for it to travel along the correct course. Modern aircraft use electronic methods of determining their rate of drift.

As in ships the compass was and still is an essential navigational instrument. However, the marine sextant proved too difficult to use and a new, slightly less accurate instrument called a BUBBLE SEXTANT was devised. Other new instruments included the ALTIMETER, AIR SPEED INDICATOR and the artificial horizon, which informs the pilot of the 'attitude' (angle compared with the horizontal) of his aircraft. Today, the pilot has the aid of an array of instruments including a rate of climb/descent indicator and a turn/slip indicator.

The artificial horizon uses a gyroscope and this device is also used in the GYROCOMPASS (see page 10), which works in conjunction with the magnetic compass. Gyroscopes are also used in automatic pilots, or INERTIAL GUIDANCE SYSTEMS (see page 10), which can fly an aircraft along a preset course, automatically correcting any changes in height or attitude.

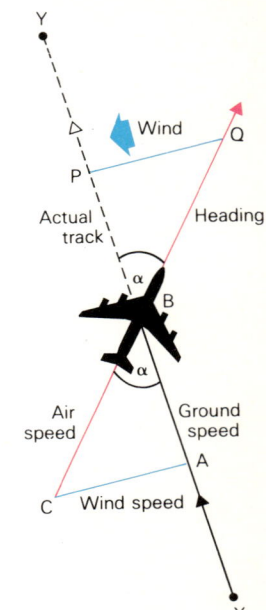

Above: Dead reckoning is used to determine the necessary compass heading of an aircraft in order to compensate for drift caused by the wind. In this instance the pilot wishes to fly from X to Y. If he knows his ground speed (AB) and the speed and direction of the wind (AC) he can plot a triangle on the map to find the airspeed and direction he must adopt (CB). The angle α is known as the angle of drift.

North American F-100 Super Sabre (America, 1954) was the first aircraft to fly faster than the speed of sound. *Engine:* Pratt and Whitney J57 turbojet, 7,700 kg thrust. *Wingspan:* 11.81 metres. *Max. speed:* 1,350 km/hour. *Crew:* 1. *Armament:* 4 20-mm cannon.

R 34 (Britain, 1919) made the first airship crossing of the Atlantic in July 1919 from East Fortune, Scotland, to Mineola, Long Island, in 110 hours. *Engines:* 5 Sunbeam Maori, 250 hp each. *Length:* 196 metres. *Diameter:* 24 metres. *Max. speed:* 100 km/hour. *Crew:* 23.

R 100 (Britain, 1929) was a highly successful airship. However, only 1 trip was

Rockwell B1 jet bomber

made, to Canada and back in July/August 1930. The R 100 was scrapped after the disastrous crash of the R 101 at Beauvais in France on October 4 1930, during a test flight (47 out of the 54 people on board were killed). *Engines:* 6 Rolls Royce Condor IIIA. *Length:* 219.4 metres. *Diameter:* 41.55 metres. *Max. speed:* 131 km/hour. *Crew:* 44.

Rockwell B-1 (America, 1968), a jet bomber, is the largest aircraft with variable geometry (swing wings). It can take off from small airbases and yet fly supersonically at altitude. *Engines:* 4 General Electric F101-100 turbofan, 13,610 kg thrust each. *Wingspan:* max. 41.7 metres, min. 23.8 metres. *Max. speed:* 2,135 km/hour. *Crew:* 5. *Armament:* 24-32 AGM-69B missiles, 34,020-52,614 kg of bombs.

Santos-Dumont, Alberto (1873–1932) was a Brazilian aviation pioneer who lived in Paris. He built several airships, the most famous of which was the *No. 6*. In 1898 it flew 11.3 km from St Cloud round the Eiffel Tower in Paris and back again.

Santos-Dumont 14-bis (France, 1906) was a box-kite aeroplane. It was the first European aircraft to make a controlled powered flight.

Travelling through Air

Right: Behind the cockpit of a USAF B-52 bomber the navigator and ECM operator sit at their controls. ECM stands for Electronic Counter Measures and the operator's task is to reduce the effect of enemy radar and other electromagnetic apparatus.

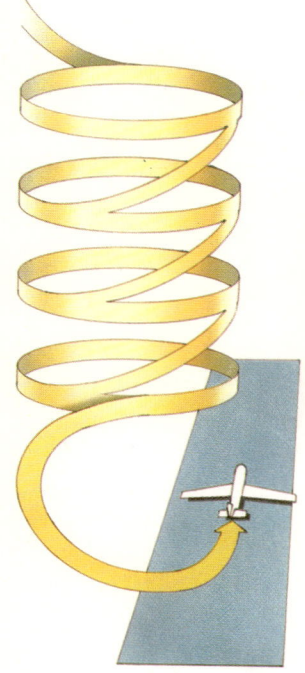

Above: At a busy airport aircraft may need to wait in a holding pattern or 'stack' before landing. Aircraft enter above those already circling and descend as others leave the holding pattern to land. The lowest holding altitude is 2,133 metres. Above this aircraft are held at 305-metre intervals, up to 8,840 metres. However, to avoid enormous delays, aircraft are usually diverted to other airports when the holding pattern reaches 6,096 metres.

Left: A Boeing 747 being loaded with passengers and luggage at an airport terminal. The 747 was the first wide-bodied jet airliner to enter service.

The first radio navigational aid used in aircraft was the D/F loop (*see page 15*). One of the first ADF (Automatic Direction Finding) systems was called VOR (Very high-frequency Omnidirectional Radio-range). This uses two transmitting stations to fix the position of an aircraft. However, it can only be used in narrow airways and additional DME (Distance Measuring Equipment) is used to show the distances of radio stations. Modern ADF systems include DECCA and LORAN (*see pages 8 and 11*). Beams of radio waves are also used in the various kinds of blind landing systems now available, which are designed for use in conditions of low or nil visibility.

Radar (*see page 14*) is used in aircraft navigation in a number of ways. DOPPLER (*see page 9*) navigational radar uses four narrow beams aimed at the ground and compares the differences in frequency between the emitted and reflected signals to determine the speed and track of the aircraft over the ground. Radar on board an aircraft is also used to detect other aircraft and storm clouds. In ground control stations radar is used to keep track of the ever-increasing air traffic, particularly near busy airports.

Guiding missiles

Guided missiles are today taking over many of the former roles of strike aircraft, as it is cheaper and safer to launch a missile from a distance and guide it to its target. The first missile used in warfare was the German V-1 flying bomb. It was guided by a magnetic compass and an automatic pilot. At a preset range the fuel supply to the jet engine was cut off and the V-1 dived to the ground. The V-2 was the first rocket-powered ballistic missile. It was aimed by calculating the correct launching angle for its trajectory to end on the target.

Since World War II there has been worldwide development of various kinds of missiles, including ballistic, anti-ballistic, air-to-air, air-to-ground, ground-to-air, anti-tank and anti-ship missiles, many of which are armed with nuclear warheads. Propulsion methods include liquid and solid-fuelled, single and multistage rockets and ram-jets (*see page 56*).

There are various guidance systems. Many early missiles were radio-controlled. Ballistic missiles rely on their trajectory and inertial guidance. Some anti-tank missiles are guided by a wire that carries electrical signals from an

---

Engine: Antoinette 8-cylinder in-line V, 50 hp. *Wingspan:* 11.2 metres. *Speed:* 40 km/hour. *Crew:* 1.
Short S.8 Calcutta (Britain, 1928) was a passenger seaplane used by Imperial Airways in the Mediterranean. *Engines:* 3 Bristol Jupiter XIF 9-cylinder radial, 540 hp each. *Wingspan:* 28.34 metres. *Cruising speed:* 148 km/hour. *Crew:* 3. *Passengers:* 15.
Sikorsky, Igor (1881–1972) was a Russian pioneer aircraft builder. After the Russian revolution of 1905 he emigrated to America and there designed aircraft and helicopters.
Sikorsky Ilya Muromets (Russia, 1915), the successor to the 4-engined *Russkii Vitiaz* (Russian Knight), was the first heavy bomber. Three were built. *Engines:* 4 Sunbeam 8-cylinder in-line V, 150 hp each. *Wingspan:* 29.8 metres. *Max. speed:* 121 km/hour. *Crew:* 4-7. *Armament:* 3-7 machine guns, 522 kg of bombs.
Sikorsky S-42 (America, 1935) was the first of the great flying boats. *Engines:* 4 Pratt and Whitney Hornet 9-cylinder radial, 750 hp each. *Wingspan:* 34.79 metres. *Cruising speed:* 274 km/hour. *Crew:* 5. *Passengers:* 32.
Sopwith F.1 Camel (Britain, 1917) was one of the most famous biplane fighters of World War I. Camels shot down 1,294 enemy aircraft. *Engine:* Clerget 9B 9-cylinder rotary, 130 hp. *Wingspan:* 8.53 metres. *Max. speed:* 185 km/hour at 2,000 metres. *Crew:* 1. *Armament:* 2 forward-firing, synchronized machine guns.
Southern Cross (Holland, 1928) was the Fokker F VIIb-3m that on May 31 set out on the first crossing of the Pacific. Charles Kingsford Smith, with a 3-man crew, completed the journey from San Francisco to Brisbane in 83 hours 28 minutes. *Engines:* 3 Wright Whirlwind 9-cylinder radial, 300 hp each. *Wingspan:* 21.71 metres. *Cruising speed:* 178 km/hour. *Crew:* 2. *Passengers:* 8-10.
Spirit of St Louis, Ryan NYP (America, 1927) was the aircraft flown by Charles Lindbergh on his solo non-stop crossing of the Atlantic in 1927. The journey from Mineola, New York, to Le Bourget, France, took 33

Short S8 Calcutta flying boat

Left: The American ALCM (Air Launched Cruise Missile). This missile requires no aiming; it is merely released from the aircraft and then flies to its target under the control of a computer program. It is powered by a turbofan engine and can fly at tree-top level, avoiding obstacles and enemy radar and defences.

Below left: An ALCM under trial, just after being launched from a Boeing B-52 bomber low over the desert.

optical sight. Some missiles home in on the infra-red (heat) rays of their targets. Others home in on radar pulses emitted either from a ground station or their own radar systems and reflected from the target. Laser and television guidance systems are also used.

The latest type of missile, and the most difficult to combat, is the cruise missile, such as the Boeing ALCM (Air-Launched Cruise Missile) and the US Navy Tomahawk. Powered by turbofan engines, both these missiles can fly a precise course to their targets at tree-top level, avoiding radar. They are guided by a computer program that enables them to avoid defence positions and follow the terrain, continuously comparing it to the information in the computer.

Navigation in space

When a satellite is launched into space it goes into orbit around the Earth. Its position is monitored at all times by ground stations, which use radio beams to follow its track. The satellite remains in its orbit owing to the combined

---

hours 39 minutes. *Engine:* Wright Whirlwind J-5-C 9-cylinder radial, 200 hp. *Wingspan:* 14.02 metres. *Cruising speed:* 180 km/hour. *Crew:* 1.

Supermarine Spitfire (Britain, 1936) was one of the most famous aircraft of World War II and over 20,300 were built in about 30 versions. One of the fastest was the 1944 Mk. XIV. *Engine:* Rolls Royce Griffon 65 12-cylinder V, 2,050 hp. *Wingspan:* 11.22 metres. *Max. speed:* 721 km/hour at 7,900 metres. *Crew:* 1. *Armament:* 2 20-mm cannon, 4 machine guns, 454 kg of bombs.

Supersonic flight begins when an aircraft exceeds the speed of sound. As an aircraft moves through the air it creates disturbances. Below the speed of sound these form a pattern of pressure waves continually moving away from the aircraft at the speed of sound. Above the speed of sound the aircraft leaves the pressure waves behind and a cone-shaped shock wave forms. As the shock wave passes a listener on the ground he hears a 'sonic boom'. The shock wave is an additional source of DRAG and supersonic aircraft are specially designed to reduce this.

T Tupolev ANT-9/M-17 (Russia, 1932) was a successful passenger transport. *Engines:* 2 M-17 12-cylinder V, 680 hp each. *Wingspan:* 23.73 metres. *Cruising speed:* 175 km/hour. *Crew:* 2. *Passengers:* 9.

Tupolev Tu 144 (Russia, 1968) was the first supersonic airliner to fly (Dec. 31 1968). *Engines:* 4 Kuznetsov NK-144 turbofan, 20,000 kg thrust each. *Wingspan:* 28.80 metres. *Max. cruising speed:* 2,500 km/hour at 17,000 metres. *Crew:* 3-4. *Passengers:* 140.

V Vickers Vimy (Britain, 1918) was designed as a bomber, but later versions were used as commercial transports. On June 14-15 1919 John Alcock and Arthur Whitten Brown made the first non-stop Atlantic cros-

Spirit of St Louis

Travelling through Air 61

Left: The Astronaut Manoeuvering Unit tested on Gemini 9 in 1966. On the astronaut's back is a life-support, communications, propulsion and control system. An emergency system is at the front. Controls for the 12 small jets are on the arm rests.

Right: The interior of an Apollo command module showing the astronauts at the controls used for navigating the spacecraft.

effects of the Earth's gravity and its own speed.

The pull of gravity is insufficient to control satellites that orbit thousands of kilometres away from Earth. One method of controlling such satellites is by using a system of photoelectric cells and a suitably positioned shade. The cells are locked on the Sun or a star and if the satellite wanders off course, the shade moves in between the cells and the light source. Small rockets on the satellite then correct its position. A similar system is used on a satellite nearer the Earth to keep its solar power cells facing the Sun.

Before sending a spacecraft to the Moon or a planet the course has to be worked out very carefully. This is because such destinations are moving through space. Therefore the spacecraft has to be aimed at a point some distance ahead of the planet's position at take-off.

An unmanned spacecraft is navigated by the ground station, using information sent back by the spacecraft's instruments. In a manned spacecraft the astronauts keep a constant check on their position. When orbiting the Earth, tracking stations send information by radio. Deeper in space navigation is accomplished by using inertial guidance systems and sextants and special telescopes to observe stars and planets. The information they provide is fed into computers, which inform the pilot of any course changes necessary.

---

sing. They flew their Vickers Vimy from St John's, Newfoundland, to Clifden, Ireland, in 16 hours 27 minutes. *Engines:* 2 Rolls Royce Eagle VIII 12-cylinder in-line V, 360 hp each. *Wingspan:* 20.47 metres. *Max. speed:* 166 km/hour. *Crew:* 3. *Armament* (removed for the Atlantic crossing): 2-4 machine guns, 1,123 kg of bombs.
Vickers Wellington (Britain, 1938) was the RAF's main bomber at the beginning of World War II. *Engines:* 2 Bristol Pegasus XVIII 9-cylinder radial, 1,000 hp each. *Wingspan:* 26.26 metres. *Max. speed:* 378 km/hour at 4,700 metres. *Crew:* 6. *Armament:* 6 machine guns, 2,000 kg of bombs.
Vickers-Armstrong Vis-

Vickers Wellington

count (Britain, 1948) was the first successful turbo-prop airliner. *Engines:* 4 Pratt and Whitney Rolls Royce Dart propeller-turbines, 1,740 hp each. *Wingspan:* 28.56 metres. *Cruising speed:* 521 km/hour. *Passengers:* 40-47.
Voisin, Charles (1882–1912) and Gabriel (1886–) were French pioneer aircraft builders.

W Whittle, Sir Frank (1907–) is the British designer of the jet engine. In 1937 he ran the first turbojet and a later version of this jet powered the GLOSTER METEOR.

Z Zeppelin, Ferdinand von (1838–1917) was a German airship builder. His first rigid airship, the *Luftschiff Zeppelin* I (LZ 1) flew in 1900.
Zeppelin (Staaken) R VI (Germany, 1917) was a large heavy bomber used to bomb London towards the end of World War I. *Engines:* 4 Mercedes D IVa 6-cylinder in-line, 260 hp each. *Wingspan:* 42.2 metres. *Max. speed:* 129 km/hour. *Crew:* 7. *Armament:* 4-7 machine guns, 2,000 kg of bombs.

The hovercraft is one of the most adaptable of all forms of transport, because it can travel over land and water. The air-cushion principle has many applications. It has even been used for lawn mowers.

Hovercraft and Hydrofoils

Right: The SR-N4 Mk. III, or Super 4, is the world's largest hovercraft. It is 56 metres long, 28 metres wide and fully loaded weighs over 300 tonnes. It is powered by 4 turboprop engines which drive the lift fans and propellers via gears. The craft is steered by movements of the propeller pylons and the 2 tail fins.

Man has continually tried to achieve higher and higher speeds on land, in the air and on water. Streamlining and powerful engines are the main methods of increasing speed and these work well for cars, trains and aeroplanes. Boats, however, have to contend with the 'stickiness' or viscosity (resistance to flow) of water. Bow and stern waves and the friction between water and the hull all tend to slow a boat down. Speed-boats, which at high speeds remove all but their sterns from the water, solve this problem to some extent, but are extremely uncomfortable. Hovercraft and hydrofoils solve the problem by having hulls that rise completely clear of the water, and so provide comfortable high-speed travel.

Hovercraft

A hovercraft is the most versatile of all forms of transport. It rides on a cushion of air and so can go almost anywhere, over land and water.

Reference

A **ACT-100,** built by Arctic Engineers and Construction, is a 250-tonne air-cushion transporter. When it was first towed slowly across ice it was found to act as an icebreaker. The air-cushion depressed the water beneath the ice which thus lost its support and cracked. This principle is now used to allow conventional ships to pass through ice. An air cushion is pushed ahead of the ship and a plough-like deflector pushes the broken ice to the sides.

Air-cushion landing systems (ACLS) are used on some aircraft. The first of these was the Lake LA-4 single-engined light amphibious aircraft built by Bell Aerospace. It has a doughnut-shaped bag skirt, from which the air escapes through thousands of tiny holes. These can be sealed to allow the craft to float.

B **Bell,** Alexander Graham (1847–1922), the American inventor, under a licence acquired from FORLANINI, built a number of 'hydrodromes' in America. One of these set a new world water-speed record of 114.03 km/hour. It was a torpedo-shaped craft with a pair of wings. It had 4 hydrofoils, 1 under each wing, 1 at the bow and 1 at the stern, and 2 air-propellers were mounted on the wings.

Boeing PGH-2 Tucumcari was the US Navy's first hydrofoil gunboat. It has sideways retracting foils and, propelled by water-jets, its top speed is 72 km/hour. Improved versions of the Tucumcari have been built, including the PHM (patrol hydrofoil missile). The Boeing Jetfoil is a 106-tonne commercial hydrofoil propelled by water-jets. Its top speed is 83 km/hour and it has a carrying capacity of 250 passengers. Both the PHM and Jetfoil have stern main foils that can be retracted by swinging them backwards.

Alexander Bell

F **Forlanini,** Enrico (1848–1930), an Italian helicopter and airship pioneer, built the first successful hydrofoil in 1905. His canoe-shaped craft, which he called a hydro-aeroplane, was equipped with 3 sets of ladder-foils, 2 in front and 1

Hovercraft and Hydrofoils

The idea of a craft riding on an air-cushion was thought of many years ago. For example, in 1879 John Thorneycroft, a British naval architect, patented the idea of a vessel riding on 'a layer of air between the bottom of the vessel and the surface of the water'. However, the technology of the time was not sufficiently advanced for him to be able to achieve this. Many inventors took up the idea, but it was not until the 1950s that the problem of keeping the air-cushion in place was solved. In 1954 Sir Christopher Cockerell, an English engineer, tried an experiment with two coffee tins, one inside the other, and an industrial drier. He discovered that forcing the air through the gap in between the tins provided an air curtain that created and maintained a central air-cushion. Using this principle, now called the annular jet, he designed the first workable hovercraft, the SR-N1, which was completed in 1959.

Small hovercraft can use Cockerell's system, but air-cushions produced in this way do not give large hovercraft sufficient clearance over obstacles. This problem was solved by adding a flexible skirt as an extension of the annular jet. It was soon discovered that this arrangement increased the clearance by up to 10 times, and the skirt automatically adjusted itself over waves or rough ground. In addition, the ring of spray around the hovercraft was found to be considerably reduced.

The air-cushion on a hovercraft is produced by one or more large fans. The main forms of forward propulsion include air-propellers, water-propellers and water-jets. Steering is achieved by rudders, either in the airstream generated by air-propellers or in the water as in a conventional boat.

Hovercraft are not only used for high speed travel over water, but also for carrying loads in factories, along roads and across swamps and ice (*see* ACT-100, VOYAGEUR). Some aircraft are fitted with AIR-CUSHION LANDING SYSTEMS so that they can land and take off almost anywhere. HOVERTRAINS are also being designed.

Hydrofoils

A stationary hydrofoil looks, at first glance, just like any other boat, with a hull that floats in the water. However, below the waterline there are foils. These have the same cross-sectional shape

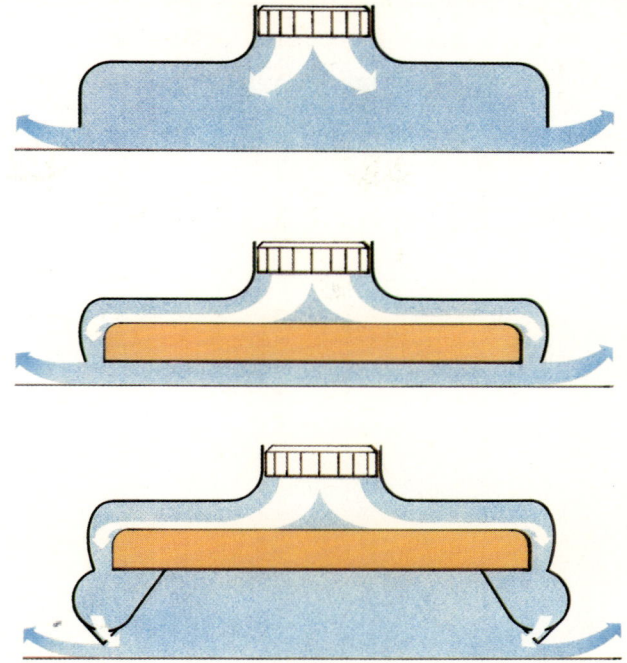

Left: The open plenum arrangement uses a single large chamber which is kept filled with air under pressure. However, this arrangement requires a considerable amount of power to maintain sufficient pressure.

Left: Sir Christopher Cockerell's design used a peripheral, or annular, jet in which air is pumped round the edge of the hovercraft. The air cushion under the whole craft is maintained using much less power.

Left: The addition of a flexible skirt to the peripheral jet arrangement increased the clearance of the hovercraft by about ten times. As a result hovercraft could negotiate rougher water or ground and became generally more useful.

Left: A fixed sidewall type of hovercraft is also known as a CAB (Captured Air Bubble) ship. It has a flexible skirt at the front and the fixed sidewalls effectively seal in the air cushion. They are more economical than hovercraft with flexible sidewalls, but they can only travel over water.

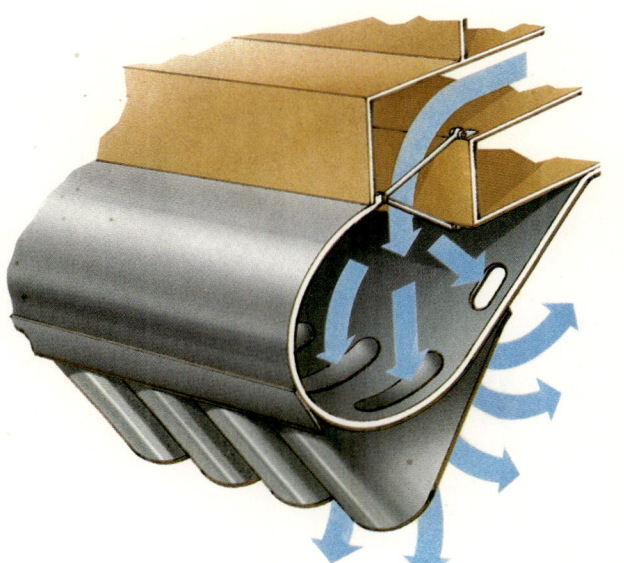

Left: A common type of skirt is one with a flexible bag to which flexible projections, known as fingers, are attached. The fingers make contact with the surface and form a seal round the air cushion. The advantage of using fingers is that if one gets pushed upwards by an obstacle or becomes damaged, the efficiency of the other fingers remains unaffected. Hovercraft with this type of skirt are comfortable to ride in and can travel at relatively high speeds in rough conditions.

---

behind, and was powered by fore and aft air propellers. It could reach speeds of up to 70 km/hour.

Grumman AGEH-1 Plainview hydrofoil

G **Grumman AGEH-1 Plainview** is the world's largest hydrofoil. An experimental ASW (anti-submarine warfare) craft, it weighs 320 tonnes and has fully-submerged foils that can be retracted sideways.

H **Hovertrains**, or tracked air-cushion vehicles (TACV), such as the Bertin Aerotrain being developed in France, will run on T-shaped guideways. They may be propelled by turbines or LINEAR ELECTRIC MOTORS (*see page 39*). Speeds of over 480 km/hour have been forecast for hovertrains.

Hydrofin was invented by Sir Christopher Hook, a British organ builder, in the 1940s. It consists of a feeler arm projecting forward with a subfoil at the front end. Attached to the subfoil, which rides clear of the water, is a heel or sensor flap, which rides on the waves. Movement of this sensor is passed to the feeler arm and thence to the main foil via linkages. Thus the pitch of the main foil is continually altered to meet each wave at the angle that keeps it at the required depth.

L **Ladder-foils** are arranged in tiers, like the rungs of a ladder. A ladder-foil is a form of SURFACE-PIERCING FOIL, and rolling and pitching are automatically controlled. If the ladder becomes more submerged, more foils generate lift and the ladder is pushed upwards again. However, flat foils have the disadvantage that a sudden drop in the amount of lift occurs as each foil breaks the surface. This problem is overcome by using foils which have a V-shape.

S **SR-Ns** were the first series of hovercraft to be

Hovercraft and Hydrofoils

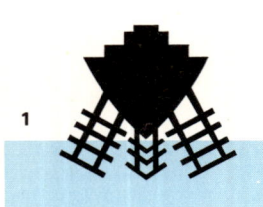

Above: Four types of hydrofoil.
1. Ladder V-foils in a conventional, or aeroplane, arrangement, with two foils at the front and a single foil at the rear. In some hydrofoils this arrangement is reversed and is called a canard arrangement.
2. V-foils arranged in tandem, a common form of surface-piercing hydrofoil.
3. Fully-submerged foils in tandem. The angle at which the foils meet each wave is controlled electronically to prevent the craft pitching backwards and forwards.
4. Fully-submerged foils in a conventional arrangement.

Below: The Grumman PGH-1 Flagstaff is a hydrofoil specially designed for the US Navy as a gunboat. This one is in operation with the coastguard and lacks guns. The design of this hydrofoil provides an unusual stability in rough seas, even at speeds of over 90 km/hour. The craft is 9.27 metres long and weighs about 71 tonnes. It has 3 fully-submerged, retractable foils and a Z-drive from the engine which is linked to a propeller on the rear foil.

Right: A Boeing Jetfoil, propelled by water jets. Two pumps drive water out through backward pointing nozzles. The pumps are operated by gas turbine engines and each one delivers over 101,300 litres of water a minute and has a thrust of over 8,100 kg. The Jetfoil weighs 108 tonnes and cruises at about 83 km/hour. It has an automatic stabilizing system and the control surfaces are computer-operated. The foils are retractable.

as a wing and behave in water in exactly the same way as a wing does in air (*see page 52*). At low speeds the hull moves through the water in the ordinary way, but as the hydrofoil increases speed, the foils generate lift and the hull rises out of the water.

The first full-sized hydrofoil craft was built by Enrico FORLANINI and tried out on Lake Maggiore in 1905. In 1918, Alexander BELL, the inventor of the telephone, built a craft in America that established a new water-speed record of over 114 kilometres per hour. Despite this achievement, interest in hydrofoils began to wane, due partly to lack of experience with lightweight engines and hulls and partly to lack of support from governments. However, in 1927 Baron Hanns von Schertel, a German engineer, designed the first hydrofoil stable enough to be used in rough weather.

Schertel used the V-foil, or dihedral SURFACE-PIERCING configuration. The advantage of this type of foil is that rolling and pitching are automatically controlled. Various types of surface-piercing foil are used today, including W-shapes and trapeze arrangements. However, the very stability of a surface-piercing foil makes it unsuitable for use in heavy seas, because the craft tends to follow the contours of high waves. Thus, surface-piercing foils are used mostly on inland waters, while sea-going craft use fully submerged foils.

Fully submerged foils do not have a natural stability and so have to be 'instructed' how to behave. The first method of doing this was a mechanical system called the HYDROFIN, devised by Christopher Hook in the 1940s. Today, most submerged foils are controlled electronically using radar, sonar and gyroscopes.

Most hydrofoils are powered by diesel engines. Power is transmitted to the propellers by inclined shafts, V-drives or Z-drives, which are all different methods of linking the engine to a propeller far beneath the hull. Some hydrofoils use water-jet propulsion systems.

---

built. The initials stand for Saunders Roe-Nautical, who built the SR-N1 according to Sir Christopher Cockerell's design. Launched in 1959, it was 9.14 metres long and 7.31 metres wide, with a top speed of 46 km/hour. Two long ducts provided the propulsion jets and it was steered by two tall rudders. In July 1959, it crossed the English Channel. Westland Aircraft, who took over Saunders Roe in 1962, built the SR-N2. This improved hovercraft was equipped with a skirt and two air-propellers set in line with a single rudder behind them. It could carry 70 passengers at a speed of 129 km/hour. The largest SR-N is the SR-N4. Five of these 200-tonne hovercraft, with cruising speeds of 111 km/hour are used to operate car/passenger ferries across the English Channel.

Surface-piercing foils have the advantage that rolling and pitching are corrected automatically. If the craft rolls to one side, more foil area becomes submerged, more lift is therefore generated and the craft is pushed upright again. In the same way if the bow pitches forward, the bow foil generates more lift and the bow is raised again. See also LADDER-FOIL.

V **Voyageur**, built by Bell Aerospace (Canada), is a workhorse air-cushion vehicle in use in northern Canada. Basically a flat platform on an air-cushion propelled by two air propellers, it can haul loads of 25 tonnes at speeds of up to 87 km/hour. The ice-breaking capabilities of fast-moving air-cushion vehicles were discovered during its trials. The craft produces standing waves in the ice half a length astern and the ice cracks at the wavecrests. The 12-metre wide platform can leave a trail of broken ice 36-metres wide. There are plans to use an air-cushion vehicle as a pipe-laying vessel in ice-bound waters.

Voyageur air cushion vehicle

Index

Page numbers in **bold** type refer to the reference sections. Page numbers in *italics* refer to the illustrations.

A
ACT-100, **62**
Abt, Roman, **33**, 44
Accelerator, **17**
Ader, Clement, **49**, 50
Aerofoils, 52
Aft, 6
 Fore-and-, 10
Aileron, 53, *53*
Air cooled engines, 17
Air cushion, **62**, *62*
Air speed indicator, 49
Aircraft, 50–58
 Navigation, 58–59
Airliner,
 Boeing, **49–50**, *50*
 Concorde, **54–55**
 de Havilland, **51–52**
 Douglas, **52**
 Farman Goliath, **53**
 Handley Page, **54**, *54*
 Lockheed Tristar, **56**, *56*
 Tupolev, **60**
 Viscount, **61**
Airlines, 55
Airships, 50
 Graf Zeppelin, **54**
 Hindenburg, **55**, *55*
 R34 and 100, **58**
Alternator, 22
Altimeter, 49
Alweg monorail, 42
America,
 Car industry in, 21
 Discovery of, 10–11
 Railways in, 36, *39*
Antifreeze, 17
Arab,
 Dhow, *9*
 Kamal, *10*
Arcera, 3
Ark Royal, 14
Arorae, Isle of, 9
Arthur Kill Bridge, **33**
Articulated steam locomotives, **33**
Artificial horizon, 58
Asdic, **6**, 16
Assembly line, 24–25, *24–25*
Astrolabe, **6**
Astronaut, **61**
Audi NSU, *24*
Austin 7, **17**, *17*
Austin 18/24, *20*
Automatic transmission, **17**, 26
Avro F, **49**, *49*
Avro Lancaster, **49**
Axle, 3

B
Backstaff, **6**
Bacon, Roger, 49
Ball bearings, **17**
Ballast, 46
Ballistic missiles, 59
Balloons, 49–50, *50*
Bardon (1901), *19*
Barge, horse-drawn, *31*
Barouche, **3**, *3*
Battery, **17**, *27*, 28
Battleship, **6**, *6*
 SMS *Rheinland*, *15*
Bayeux tapestry, *9*
Bayonne Bridge, **17**, *17*
Beam bridge, *28*, 29
Bearings (in navigation), 10, 13
Bearings (in wheels), **17**
Bell, Alexander, **62**, *62*
Benoist XIV, **49**
Benz, Karl, 17, 21
 Velo, **18**, *20*
Berlin coaches, *3*
Best Friend of Charleston, **33**, *33*
Bicycle, **22**, 23, *23*, 24
 Derailleur gear, **20**
 Epicyclic gears, **20**
 Humber, **22**
 Moulton, **23**, *23*
 Penny farthing, *22*, 24, *24*
Big end, 18
Biremes, **7**, 8
Blenkinsop, John, 35, 43
Blériot XI, 52, *52*
Blucher, **33**
Blue Train, **34**
Boats,
 Cog, *7*
 Early, 6–7
 Paddle, 13, 14
 Papyrus, *7*
 Steam, 14
Boeing,
 80A/247, **49**
 707/747, **50**, *50, 58*
 Flying Fortress, **49**
 Hydrofoil, **62**
 Superfortress, **50**
Bomber, 56
 Avro Lancaster, **49**
 Consolidated Liberator, **51**
 Flying Fortress, **49**

Handley Page, **54**
Heinkel, **55**
Junkers, **55**
Rockwell B-1, **58**, *58*
Sikorsky Ilya Muromets, **59**
Superfortress, **50**
Wellington, **61**, *61*
Brakes, **18**, *18*, 21, *26*, 27, *27*, 28
 Hand, **22**, *27*
 Railway, **34**
 Servo-assisted, **25**
Briare Canal, **30**
Bridge(s), **22**, 24–25, *28*, 29, 33, *38*, 45
 Bayonne, **17**, *17*
 Britannia, **34**, *34*
 Cantilever, **25**, *25*, 28, 45
 Forth Rail/Road, **21**, *21*, 37
 Golden Gate, **22**, *22*
 Suspension, **22**, *22*, 23, 28, 45
 Sydney Harbour, 45
 Tay, 46, *46*
 Trestle, 44
Bridgewater Canal, **30**, *30*, 32
Bristol Beaufighter, **50**
Britannia Bridge, **34**, *34*
British Rail Advanced Passenger Train, 48, *48*
Brougham, 3
Brown, Sam, 17
Brunel,
 Isambard Kingdom, **34**, 36, 46
 Sir Marc Isambard, **35**
Bubble sextant, 50
Buggy, 3
Bullet train, 48, *48*

C
Cab,
 Hansom, **4**
 Railway, *43*
Cable car, **23**
Cabot, John, 11
Cabriolet, 3
Caissons, 32
Calabash, sacred, **14**
Caledonian Ship Canal, **30**
Cam, shaft, **18**
Camber, 18
Canadian, **35**
Canal du Midi, **30**
Canals, 30–32
 Bridgewater, **30**, *30*
 Lock, **31**
Canoes, 9
 Dug-out, **9**, *9*
Cantilever bridge, **25**, *25*, 29, 45
Capacity, 18
Capsule, space, *61*
Car, *27*
 Cable, 23
 Design, 22
 Early, 17
 Electric, 23
 Industry, 21–22, 24–25
 Mechanics, 25–26
 Production line, *24–25*
Caravel, **7**, *10*
Carburettor, **18**, *19*, 21, *27*, 28
 Choke and, **19**
Carrack, **7**, *10*
Cart, Vietnamese, *4*
Carvel, 7
Cascade Tunnel, **35**
Catch-me-who-can, **35**, *35*
Cayley, Sir George, 50, *50*
Celts, 4
Centennial, **35**
Central Railway of Peru, **35**
Chairs, sedan, *5*
Chaise, 3
 Post-, *5*
Chamber lock, **30**
Channel Tunnel, *28*
Chanute, Octave, 50, *50*
Char, *3*
Chariots, 4
 Roman, *5*
Charles, Prof. Jacques, 51
Charleston, Best Friend of, **33**, *33*
Charlotte Dundas, **13**
Charts, 9–10, 13
 Twig, **16**
China,
 Clippers, **56**
 Lock, **30**
 Train, *41*
Choke, **19**
 Carburettor and, **18**, *19*
Chronometer, 12
Circuits, track, **46**, 47
Classification, **35**
Clinker, **7**
Clipper, 14
 China, **56**
Clock, marine, 12
Clutch, **19**, 26, *27*
Coaches, 5
 Berlin, 3
 Concord, **4**
 Hackney, **4**
 Mail, **5**, *5*
 Pullman, *42*
 Railway, **38**
 Stage, 5
 Steam, 17

Coachwork, *25*
Cockerell, Sir Christopher, **63**
Cockpit, *59*
Cog boat, **7**
Coil, **19**
Columbus, Christopher, **10**
Combustion, 18, 20
Comet, de Havilland, **52**
Compass, 9, 13
 Ratio, 19
Compression, 18, 20
 Ratio, 19
Concord coaches, **4**
Concorde, **54–55**
Conestoga wagons, **4**
Consolidated Liberator, **51**
Construction,
 Road, 28, *29*
 Tunnel, 44–45
Control, electronic, 47
Cook, Captain, 13
Coolant system, 25–26
 Radiator and, **25**
Coracles, 8
Corinth Canal, **30**, *30*
Corvette, **7**, *7*
Coupling, **36**, *36*
Cowcatcher, 40
Crankshaft, **20**
Crash test, *26*
Cross-staff, **7**, *12*
Crown wheel, **20**
Cruise missile, 60, *60*
Cruiser, 8
Cugnot, N. J., 17
 Steam tractor and, *17*
Curraghs, 8
Curré, 3
Curricle, 4
Curtiss, Glen, **51**
 Navy, **54**
 P40B, **51**, *51*
'Cut and cover', 44
Cylinder, engine, 18, *18*
Cylindrical projection, *12*

D
Daimler, Gottlieb, 17, 21
de Havilland, Geoffrey, **51**
 Comet, **52**
 DH4A, **51**
 Mosquito, **52**
 Tiger Moth, 52, *52*
Dead man's handle, **36**
Dead reckoning, 12, 58, *58*
Decca system, **8**, 15
Declination, **8**
Dectra system, **8**, 15
Depth sounding, 7
Der Adler, **38**
Derailleur gear, **20**
Design, car, 22, 24
Destroyer, **8**, *9*
Deviation, **9**
Dhow, *9*
Diaz, Bartholomew, 10
Diesel,
 Engine, 18, *18*, 20
 Locomotives, 40, *41*
 Rudolf, 18
Differential, **20**, 27
Diligence, *4*
Direction stones, 9
Disc brakes, **18**, *18, 27*, 28
Dished wheels, *4*
Distributor, **20**, *20*
Dock, 32
 Dry, **31**, *32*
 Floating, **31**
Döppler effect, *9*
Dornier Do 217, **52**
Douglas DC-2, **52**, *55*
Drag, 52, 53
Drake, Sir Francis, 11
Draisienne, **20**, *22*
Dreadnought, HMS, **6**
Drill, Pneumatic, 44
Drum brakes, **18**, *18, 26*, 28
Dry dock, **31**, *32*
Dug-out canoes, **9**, *9*
Dynamo, 22

E
Echo-sounder, 16
Egyptian boats, 6–7, *6–7*
Electric(al)
 Car, 23
 Locomotives, 42, *42*
 Motor, **39**, *48*
 Train, **41**
Electronics, 47
Engine, 25
 Air-cooled, **17**
 Compound, 40
 Diesel, 18, *18*
 Jet, 56–57, *56–57*
 Newcomen's, *34*
 Petrol, 18, *18*
 Steam, 33–34, 38, *38*
 Wankel, *19*
Engineering,
 Canal, 31
 Railway, 44–45, *45*
Epicyclic gear system, **20**
Equinoxes, *78*
Erie Canal, **31**, *32*
Eriksson, Leif, 9
Exhaust, 18, 20, *27*, 28
Exploration, Age of, 10–11

F
Fanbelt, *27*
Farman, Henri, **53**
 F60 Goliath, **53**
Fell system, 43
Festiniog Railway, **36**, *36*
Fiat coupé, *20*
Fighter, 56
 Bristol Beaufighter, **50**
 Curtiss P40B, **51**, *51*
 Dornier, **52**
 Focke-Wulf, **53**
 Fokker, **53**
 Gloster Meteor, **53**
 Hawker Hurricane, **54**
 Heinkel, **55**
 Junkers, **55**
 Lockheed Lightning, **56**
 Mosquito, **52**
 Mustang, **57**
 Phantom, **56**
 Sopwith Camel, **55**, *59*
 Super Sabre, **58**
 Spitfire, **60**
 Zero, **57**
Filter, *27*
Flamsteed, John, 14
Flash lock, 30
Flight, 52
 Man's attempts, 49
 Powered, 50–52
 Control surfaces, 53, *53*
 Supersonic, 57, *60*
 Path, 58
Floating dock, **31**
Flooding, mine, 34
Flying
 Hamburger, **37**
 Scotsman, **37**, *41*
Flywheel, 21
Focke-Wulf, **53**
Foils, **63**, *64, 64*
Fokker, Anthony, **53**
 Aircraft, **53**, *53*
Ford,
 Model T, 21, *21, 21*
 Fiesta, *26–27*
Fore-and-aft, 10
Forlanini, Enrico, **62**
Forth Rail/Road Bridge, **21**, *21, 37*
Four-stroke engine, 18, *18*, 25
France, railways in, 36
Frigate, **10**, *10*
Fuel, injection, 21
Funicular railways, 43

G
Galleass, **10**
Galleon, **10**, 11
Galleys, **7**, 8
 Roman, *8*
Garratt locomotives, **37**
Gauges, railway, 36–37
Gearbox, **26**, *27*
Gear(s), **21**, 26
 Derailleur, **20**
 Differential, **20**
 Epicyclic, **20**
Generator, **22**, *27*, 28
Georgetown loop, *45*
Gig, 4
Gladesville Bridge, **22**
Glasgow, HMS, *8*
Glider, 50–51, *51*
Gloster Meteor, **53**
Glückauf, 15
Golden Gate Bridge, **22**, *22*
Graf Zeppelin, **54**
Great and Little Bear, 13
Great Eastern, 13
Great Western Railway, **36**, 46
Grumman Plainview, **63**, *63–64*
Guidance system, inertial, **10**
Guided missiles, 59
Gusmao, Bartolomeu de, 49
Gyrocompass, **10**, 15
Gyroscope, 15–16, 58

H
Hackney coaches, **4**
Halifax bomber, **54**
Halley, Edmund, 13
Hamburger, Flying, **37**
Hand brake, **22**, *27*
Handley Page, **54**, *54*
Hang gliding, **51**
Hansom cabs, **4**, *4*
Harley Davidson, **22**
Harrison, John, 12
Hawaii, 9
 Sacred calabash and, **14**
 Twig charts and, **16**
Hawker Hurricane, **54**
Heinkel, **54**, 55
Helicopter, **57**, 58
Henry the Navigator, 10
Hall Gate Bridge, **38**
Hercule, **10**
Hero, 33, **38**
Herodotus, 7
Hildebrand and Wolfmüller, **22**
Hindenburg, **55**, *55*
Hobby horse, *22*, 23
Horizon, artificial, 58
Horses, 4
 Hobby, *22*, 23

Power, 23
Hovercraft, **62–63**, *62–63*
 SRNs, **63**
Hovertrain, **48**, *63*
Huey P. Long Bridge, **38**
Humber
 Bicycle, **22**
 Bridge, **23**
Hydrofin, **63**
Hydrofoils, **63–64**, *63–64*
 Forlanini and, **62**
 Principles, **64**, *64*

I
Icarus, 49, *49*
Indian Pacific, **38**, *38*
Industry, car, 21–22, 24–25
Inertial guidance system, **10**
Injection, fuel, 21
Internal combustion engines, 18, *18*, 20
Iron,
 Rails, 33
 Ships, 14
Isogonic charts, 13

J
Jenatzy, Camille, 23
Jet,
 Aircraft, **53–56**, 57
 Engines, 56–57, *56–57*
 Jumbo, *58*
Joint, universal, 26, *28*
Jumbo Jet, *58*
Junkers, 55, *55*

K
Kalia, 9
Kamal, *10*
Kanmon Tunnel, **38**
Key West Extension, **38**
Kicking Horse Pass, **39**
King George V, **39**
Kingsford-Smith, Charles, 56
 Southern Cross and, **59**
Knocking, 23
Knot, **12**

L
Ladder-foils, **63**
Lambretta, *22*
Landau, *4*
Languedoc Canal, **30**
Lateen rig, *10*
Latitude, **11**, 12
 Sextant and, **15**
Leonardo da Vinci, 49
de Lesseps, Ferdinand,
 Panama Canal and, **31**, *31*
 Suez Canal and, **32**
Levassor, Emile, 21
Levitation, magnetic, **39**, *48*
Lilienthal, Otto, 50
 Glider and, **51**
Lindbergh, Charles, 56
 Spirit of St Louis and, **59**, *60*
Line, log and, **11**
Linear electric motor, **39**, *48*
Liverpool and Manchester Railway, **36**, *37*, 38
Lock, canal, 30–31, *31*
Lockheed,
 Lightning, **56**
 Tristar, **56**, *56*
Locomotion, **39**, *39*
Locomotives, 35, *38*, 38, 39–40
 Articulated steam, **33**
 Centennial, **35**
 Classification, **35**
 Diesel-electric, 40, *41*, 42, *42*
 Garratt, **37**
 Mallet, **40**
 Tank, 46
Log,
 Line and, **11**
 Patent, 13, *13*
Longitude, **11**, *11*, 12
Longships, 8
Loran, **11**, 15
Lorry, **22**, 22
Los Angeles freeways, *29*

M
McAdam, John, *29*
McDonnell-Douglas Phantom, **56**
Mach number, **56**
Macmillan, Kirkpatrick, 23
Mack lorry, *20*
Magellan, Ferdinand, 11
Magnetic,
 Levitation, **39**, *48*
 Variation, 13, **16**
Mail coach, 5, *5*
Mallard, **40**
Manifold, **23**
Maps, Pre-Columbus, *11*
Marcus, Siegfried, 17
Marsh, Sylvester, **40**
Marshall Is., 9
Marshalling yards, 47, *47*
Matchless penny farthing, *22*
Mercator, Gerardus, 10, **11**, *12*
 Projection, *12*
Meridian, **12**
 Prime, 13
Mesopotamia, 30

Index

Messerschmitt, **56–57**, *57*
Metal fatigue, 57
Metcalf, John, 28
Michaux Velocipede, 23–24
Mile, nautical, **12**
Mines,
    Flooding, 34
    Tracks, 33, *33*
Missiles,
    Ballistic, 59
    Cruise, 60, *60*
    Guided, 59
Mistral, **40**
Mitre gates, 30–32
Mitsubishi 'Zero', 57
Monorails, 42, *43*
Mont
    Blanc tunnel, 23
    Cenis tunnel, **40**, *40*
Montgolfier brothers, 49–50, *50*
Morane-Saulnier, 57
Morris Cowley, 23, *23*
Moscow underground, 44
Mosquito, de Havilland, 52
Motor, linear electric, **39**, *48*
Motorcycles, **22**, 23, *23*, 24
Motorway, **23**, 29
Moulton bicycle, **23**, *23*
Mountain railways, 43
Mustang, 57

N
Nakajima Hayate, 57
Nao, **7**
Nautical mile, **12**
Navigation, 7–9, 12–16
    Aircraft, 58–59
    Astrolabe, **6**
    Backstaff, 6
    Cross-staff, **7**
    Decca, **8**
    Declination, **8**
    Dectra, 8
    Doppler effect, **9**
    Kamal, **10**
    Latitude, **11**
    Longitude, **11**, *11*
    Loran, **11**
    Mercator and, 10, **11–12**, *12*
    Nautical mile and, **12**
    Prince Henry, 10
    Radar and, **14**, *14*
    Sacred calabash and, 14
    Sonar and, **15**
    Space, 60–61
New River Gorge Bridge, 24
Newcomen, Thomas, **34**, *34*, 40
Nocturnal, **13**
Normandie, 14
North Star, **41**
Northern Line, **41**
Nuclear submarine, *16*

O
Observatory, Royal, **14**
Octane, 24
Octant, **13**, *13*
Odyssey, 8
Oil, Engine, 25
Orient Express, **41**
Otto, Nikolaus, 17–18
Oystermouth Railway, 33

P
Paddle boat, *13*, 14
Panama Canal, **31–32**, *31*
Panhard, Réné, 21
Pantograph, 42
Papin, Denis, **34**, 41
Papyrus boats, 6, *7*
Passenger transport, 38, **48**, *48*
Patent log, 13, *13*
Pavement, **24**, *24*
Penny farthing, **22**, 24, **24**
Penydarran, 35, **38**, 41
Peru, Central Railway of, 35
Peruvian dug-out canoe, *9*
Petrol(eum), 17
    Engine,**18**, *18*
Phaeton, **5**, *5*
Phantom, **56**
Phoenicians, 7–8
Pilatus Railway, **41**, *41*
Pinion, **20**
    Rack and, **33**, 41, 43, 44
Pinking, 23
Piston, **24**
Plug, spark, **26**, *27*
Pneumatics, 44
Points system, *37*
Polynesians, 9
    Sacred calabash and, **15**
    Twig charts and, **16**
Pont de Quebec, **25**, *25*
Port, **13**
Post-chaise, **5**
Power,
    Horse, **86**
    Steam, 33
    Steering, 27
Production line, *24–25*
Projection, **10**
    Mercator, **12**
Puffing Billy, 35, **42**
Pullman, George, **42**, *42*
Pump, steam/vacuum, 34

Q
Quadrant, **14**
Quinquiremes, **7**

R
R 34 and 100, **58**
RDF, 15
Rack rail system, **33**, *41*, 43, *43*, 44
Radar, **14**, 16, 59
    Scanner, **14**
Radiator, **25**, *27*
    Cooling system and, 25–26
Radio, 14-15
    Waves, 15–16, 59
Raeda, **5**
Raft, log, *3*
Railways, 33–48
    Brakes, **34**
    Festiniog, **36**, *36*
    Gauges, 36–37, **37**, *37*
    Horse-drawn, *35*
    Liverpool and Manchester, 36, *37*, 38
    Mountain, 43
    Pilatus, **41**, *41*
    Speed, **44**
    Stockton and Darlington, 35
Rainhill trials, 36
Rhaetian Railway, 42
Re 6/6, **42**
Rig,
    Lateen, **10**
    Square, **16**, *16*
Riggenbach, Nikolaus, **42**
Rim, **5**
Roads, 28–29
    Construction, 28, *29*
    Minor, **23**
    Motorway, **23**
    Pavement, **24**, *24*
    Primary, **25**
    Secondary, **25**
    Shoulder, **26**
    Subgrade, **27**
    Trunk, **28**
Rocket, Stephenson's, 35–36, *36–37*, **39**, 42
Rockwell B-1, **58**, *58*
Roller, Bearings, **17**
Roman
    Chariot, *5*
    Galley, *8*
    Roads, 28
    Transport, 4
Rotherhithe Tunnel, *35*
Rotor blades, 58
Royal George, **43**
Royal Observatory, **14**

S
SMS *Rheinland*, 15
SRN hovercraft, *63–64*
Sails, 10–11, 14
St Gotthard Tunnel, **43**, *43*
St Lawrence Seaway, **32**, *32*
St Louis, Spirit of, **59**, 60
St Pancras Station, *44*
Salamis, Battle of, 8
Santos-Dumont, Alberto, 52, **58**
Satellite, 60–61
Sault Sainte Marie Bridge, **25**
Savery, Thomas, **34**, **43**
Scanner, radar, *14*
School, navigation, 9–10
Scotsman, Flying, **37**, 41
Seajet hydrofoil, *64*
Seaplane,
    Benoist XIV, **49**
    China Clippers, **56**
    Navy Curtiss, **54**
    Short Calcutta, **59**, *59*
    Sikorsky S-42, **59**
Sedan chairs, **5**
Servo-assisted brakes, 25
Severn Tunnel, **43**
Sextant, *12*, 13, **15**
    Bubble, **50**
Shaft drive, **26**
Shield, tunnel, 44
Shinkansen Hikari, **43**, *48*
Ship-of-the-line, **15**, *15*
Ships, 6–16
    Canal, **30**, 32
    Steam, 35
Short Calcutta, **59**, *59*
Shoulder, **26**
Sidecar, 24
Siemens, Dr. Ernst von, **43**
Signals, 44, 47
    Box, *44*, 47
Sikorsky, Igor, **59**
Sikorsky (aircraft), **59**
Silencer, **26**, *27*
Simplon Tunnel, **44**
Sleeper, 46, *46*
Solenoid switch, **26**
Sonar, **15**, 16
Sopwith Camel, **54**, *59*
Southern Cross, **59**
Space
    Capsule controls, **61**
    Navigation, 60–61
Spark plug, **26**, *27*
Speed,
    Air, 49
    Mach, **56**
Rail, **44**
    Supersonic, **60**
Speedometer, **26**, *27*
Spices, 10
Spitfire, **60**
Spoked wheel, 4, *5*
Sprague, Frank, 42
Sprocket, **27**
Square rig, **16**, *16*
Stacking, 59
Stagecoaches, **5**
Starboard, **16**
Starley,
    J.K., 24
    James, 23
    Rover, 22
Starter motor, **27**
Steam
    Coaches, 17, 35
    Engine, 33–34
    Locomotives, **33**, 38, *38*, 39
    Pump, 34
    Ship, *13*, 14, **35**
    Tractor, 17
Steering, 27, **27**, *27*
Stephenson, George, 35–37, 39, **45**
    Blucher and, **33**
    Locomotion and, **39**, *39*
    Rocket and, 35–36, *36–37*
Stephenson, Robert, **45**, *45*
Stockton and Darlington Railway, 35
Stone,
    Direction, **9**
    Roads, 28
Stonehenge, 3
Subgrade, **27**
Submarines, 14
    Nuclear, 16
Suez Canal, **32**, *32*
Sumerian transport, 3–4
Super Sabre, **58**
Supercharger, **27**
Superheating, **39**, **45**
Supersonic flight, 57, **60**
Supertanker, *16*
Surface-piercing foils, 64, *64*
Surrey Iron Railway, 33
Suspension, 5, 27, **27**, *27*
    Bridge, **22**, *22*, **23**, *28*, **29**, *29*
    Wheels, 23–24
Swing wings, 57
Synchromesh, 26
Sydney Harbour Bridge, **45**, *45*

T
Tank, engine, **39**, **46**
Tay Bridge, **46**, *46*
Tees Bridge, **46**
Telford, Thomas, 29, **30**
Tender, **46**
Terra Australis Incognita, **11**
Tide, 8
Tiger Moth, **52**, *52*
Tin Lizzie, 21, **21**, *21*
Tonkiaka, 9
Tracks, rail, 33, *33*, 44, 46, *46*
    Circuits, **46**, 47
Tractor, steam, *17*
Trade, 10
Trains, *see* Railways
Trams, 23
Trans-Siberian Express, **47**
Transmission, automatic, **17**, 26, **27**, *28*
    Epicyclic gears and, **20**
Transport,
    Air, 49–61
    Early, 3–5
    Rail 33–48
    Road, 17–29
    Water, 6–16, 30–32
Traverse board, 12, **16**, *16*
Trestle railway, 42, *44*
Tresuaget, Pierre, 28
Trevithick, Richard, 17, 35, *35*, 38, **46**
    Road Passenger Locomotive, *46*
Triremes, **7**, *8*
Tunnel, 29
    Channel, *28*
    Construction, 44–45
    Kanmon, 38
    Mont Blanc, 23
    Mont Cenis, **40**, *40*
    Rotherhithe, *35*
    St Gotthard, **43**, *43*
    Severn, **43**
    Simplon, **44**
    Yerbo Bueno Island, 29
Tupolev, **60**
Twig charts, **16**
Two-stroke cycle, **28**
Tyres, 21, 24, **28**

U
U-boat, *14*
Ultrasound, 16
Underground railways, 42
    Moscow, 44
Union Pacific Big Boys, **47**
Universal joint, 26, **28**
Universe Ireland, 16

V
V-1 and 2, 59

Vacuum pump, 34
Valves, **29**, 48
Variation, magnetic, 13, **16**
Velo, Benz, **18**, *20*
Ventilation, tunnel, 45
Verrazano Narrows, **29**, *29*
Vertical take-off, 57–58
Vespucci, Amerigo, 11
Vickers Vimy, **60**
Victoria Falls Bridge, **48**
Vietnamese cart, *3*
Vikings, 8–9
Vinland, 9
Viscount airliner, **61**
Voisin, Charles, **61**
Volkswagen Beetle, *20*
Voyageur, **64**, *64*
Vulcanizing, **4**

W
Wagons,
    Conestoga, **4**
    Early, 3–5
Wankel engine, *19*, 20
Warfare, air, 55–56
Water, transport, 62
Watt, James, 34, **48**
    Steam governor, **48**
Waves, radio, 15–16
Welland Canal, 32, *32*
Wellington bomber, **61**, *61*
Wheels, 3, *3*, 4
    Crown, **20**
    Dished, **4**
    Flanged, 33
    Rim, **5**
    Spoked, 4, **5**, *5*, 23
    Suspension, 23–24
Whirlicote, **5**
Whittle, Sir Frank, **61**
Winds, sailing, 9
Wings, 50, 52–53
    Flight control surfaces, *53*
    Swing, 57
Wolseley bus, **20**
World War II aircraft, 56
Wright, Wilbur and Orville, 50–51
    Flyer, *51*
Wuppertal Railway, 42

Z
Zambezi Bridge, **39**, **48**
Zenith, **16**
Zeppelin, 50, **61**
    Count von, **61**
    Graf, **54**
Zero, Mitsubishi, **57**

Acknowledgements

Contributing artists
Marian Appleton, Charles Bannerman, Raymond Brown, Chris Forsey, Ivan Lapper, Jim Marks, Nigel Osborne, Alan Suttie, Ken Warner.

The Publishers also wish to thank the following:
Allsport/Don Morley 23T
W. David Askham 41TR, 52T
Australian Information Service 38B
Barnaby's 30B, 44T, 46C, 61T
Bell Aerospace 64B
Boeing Aerospace Limited 60T, 60C, 64TR
British Airways 54B, 59B
British Transport Films 48TR, 48C
Camera Press 28T
Camera Press/J. H. Pickerell 59T
Camera Press/L. Willinger 29C
J. Allan Cash 22B, 25B
Central Office of Information 57L
Cooper Bridgeman Library 35T, 37T
R. J. Davis Contents BR, 55T
Daily Telegraph Colour Library/A. Howarth 58T
Robert Estall 32T
Mary Evans Picture Library 7B, 9B, 10B, 12B, 15B, 55B, 62B
Fiat 27B
Ford Motor Co. Ltd 26T, 26B
Fotomas Index 13T, 50T
James Gilbert 53B, 56B, 57B, 60B
Grand Western Houseboat Co. 31T
Sally and Richard Greenhill 23C, 41TL, 43C
Grumman Aerospace Corporation 63B, 64TL
Hawker Siddeley Aviation Ltd 49B
Hoverlloyd 62T
Alan Hutchinson Library Contents, 9C
Michael Holford 5C, 9T, 11T, 16BR
Japan Information Centre 48TL
Mansell Collection 30T, 39C, 51TL
Ministry of Defence/Crown Copyright 6B, 8B, 52B
National Maritime Museum 13B
National Motor Museum, Beaulieu 21T (Courtesy Museu do Automoval Do Ceramulo, Portugal)
Novsti 44C
Photographic Library of Australia 45C
Photri 44BL, 46T, 47C
Picturepoint 43TR
Popperfoto 11B, 17BL, 17BR, 23BL, 29B, 50B, 51B
Raleigh Ltd 23BR
Rockwell International 58B
Rolls Royce Motors Ltd 23B
Ann Ronan Picture Library 3B, 4B, 5B, 24B, 31B, 32B, 33B, 34B, 35B, 36BL, 36BR, 37B, 39B, 40B, 41B, 42B, 43B, 44BR, 45B, 46B, 47B, 48B, 49T
Science Museum 51C
Scottish Tourist Office 21B
Seajet 64TR
Societe Nationale des Chemins de Fer (SNCF) 43TL, 47T
Spectrum 16T
Swiss National Tourist Office 42T
P.N. Trotter 39T
Vickers Ltd 61B
Volkswagen GB Ltd 24T, 25T
Walker Art Gallery, Liverpool 34T
Yachts and Yachting 16BL
Jerry Young 51TR
Zefa 14B, 57B